Kelly Simpson PERFECTLY describes the dangers take place when working with strangers and effectively constructs a plan on ways to protect yourself. Not only is this book inspiring and will leave you wanting to learn more, but the imagery will keep you on your toes!

—DR. MELISSA MARSILI

Not Today, Predator delivers practical and straightforward strategies for anyone who interacts with strangers to adopt immediately in order to greatly reduce the potential for being attacked. I never realized how often I was putting myself at risk, and this made me look at the world with a whole new perspective.

—KELLY ALLAIN,
Director of Business Development, American Road Group, Harley-Davidson

Not Today, Predator gives real-world and straightforward tactics not just for real estate agents, but **anyone** who interacts with strangers to implement immediately in order to greatly reduce the potential for being attacked.

—SERGEANT NICHOLAS HAFF,
Village of Winnebago Police Department

What Kelly Simpson reveals in this must-read book is something that can absolutely transform your awareness of safety in any field. Part compelling stories, part instructive handbook, *Not Today, Predator* is full of Mastery Skills everyone should know.

—SHIRLEY RAMOS
Ret. Chief QA Analyst, Bally Ent.

Gut Wrenching! The insights, analysis, and expertise that Kelly Simpson shares in this book are invaluable! Anyone who has ever worried about their personal safety should read *Not Today, Predator* and send your awareness level and nonverbal intelligence soaring!

—**CHERYL NELSON,**
Former COA, BlackBox Inc.

In my business as a mortgage loan officer, I work with and become friends with many real estate professionals, including the author, Kelly Simpson. Anything that can help to keep them safe so they can conduct their business is crucial. This is a must-have guide to help keep them safe!

—**MATT KENNEDY,**
Vice President Mortgage Lending, Guaranteed Rate Affinity

This one hits HOME! As a leader in this industry, it is my job to make agent safety and awareness top of mind for the agents I serve. This book will be my new go-to guide. Chilling stories and current research tell a tough story, but one that needs to be heard. The brokerage workbook is relevant and a definite must in new agent training. I'm grateful to have a companion in helping real estate agents be on the path to Mastery when it comes to the "dos and don'ts" and their safety in the field.

—**LAURA BOYER,**
Regional Vice President, Coldwell Banker Real Estate Group

NOT TODAY PREDATOR

WHAT YOU DON'T KNOW CAN KILL YOU

KELLY SIMPSON

FOREWORD BY ADORNA OCCHIALINI CARROLL

SB
PRESS

Published by StoryBuilders Press

ISBN: 978-1-954521-08-7 Paperback
ISBN: 978-1-954521-09-4 Hardback
ISBN: 978-1-954521-10-0 Ebook

First edition.

This book deals with predatory assault. While the author has taken great lengths to ensure the subject matter is dealt with in a compassionate and respectful manner, it may be troubling for some readers. Discretion is advised.

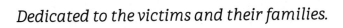

Dedicated to the victims and their families.

contents

foreword

I am your average real estate professional, and after reading *Not Today, Predator* by Kelly Simpson, I realize I am lucky to be alive.

Professionals in the real estate business are driven individuals with very busy lives. As self-employed independent contractors, we are only paid when a buyer actually buys or a seller actually sells a property. There are no guarantees. We often work countless hours, days, weeks, and months before we are able to conclude a transaction and receive a check for the services we rendered.

We get no health insurance benefits, no retirement benefits, and no taxes are taken out of the checks we receive. We must buy all of our own equipment, software, and business tools; all of those business expenses incurred are paid out of our own pocket upfront before we ever earn any money.

Additionally, that big check from the property closing belongs to the brokerage company we work for and is not ours to keep. It is divided countless ways before we finally get a much smaller check. When all is said and done, we need a lot of those smaller checks to feed our families, pay our bills, pay our taxes, and secure our own health insurance.

That is why, more often than not, we are apt to run out the door after receiving a call, email or text to work with someone we really don't know all that well or will be meeting for the first time.

People think we are rich, but those of us in the business know that is not usually the case. Many of us struggle on a commission fee schedule, but that is how the real estate industry is structured. We usually work long days, nights, and weekends as a matter of routine to earn a decent living. To attract more business, we present ourselves to the public as successful top producers, drive nice cars, and dress well—which can sometimes make us a prime target for every whack job and wing nut out there.

Reading Kelly's book was an epiphany for me. Real estate professionals generally lack the tools to protect themselves in everyday work situations. We have no idea the degree to which we are exposed, and Kelly demonstrates that fact at every turn of every page. What I appreciated most from her were the common sense Mastery Skills she provides after she describes each bone-chilling event in which a real estate professional was harmed, robbed, raped, tortured, and/or murdered.

It has been the dirty little secret in our industry. Occasionally we hear about real estate professionals that are found dead in basements, attics, or sheds in the woods, deserts, fields, or mountains. It wasn't widely publicized—just mentioned in passing by colleagues and friends of friends.

Social media and Beverly Carter's murder brought everything to the forefront for many of us. That was the first time that we as a group of professionals shined a light on the problem that professionals like me face every day when we do our job, and it is frightening for ourselves and the families that love us.

In reading the details of Kelly's book, I now realize I was one of the lucky ones. I had a close encounter with a predator in my career. Reading this book brought it all back for me—something I never shared with my family, but only discussed with students in my own classes when I teach the advanced credentials—Seller Representative Specialist (SRS) conferred by the Real Estate Business Institute (REBI) and the Accredited Buyer Representative (ABR) conferred by the National Association of Realtors (NAR).

It was a vacant property, backed up to woods at the end of a cul-de-sac in a buyers' market with tons of inventory at that price point. Some stranger called me, and I answered my phone in the car rather than allowing it to go to voicemail. He said he was from out of state and wanted to meet me at the property on the following Thursday. Against all instincts—since my normal protocol was to meet all prospective clients at the office—I agreed to do it.

Feeling uneasy, with a pit in my stomach, I called and asked my licensed assistant to meet me at the property to meet with the buyer. I had her come in her own car, wait outside, and call the license plate into the office with a description of what ended up being a blue van with no windows and New York plates (I am from Connecticut) parked on the street.

I told her to stay down at the end of the driveway in her locked car, and that if anything were to happen, she should call the police. I waited as the buyer walked up the long driveway, never opening the front door. I asked him for his name to see if it matched what he told me, and out of the corner of my eye, I saw a man in overalls and galoshes come from the fenced backyard.

I asked, "Who is that, and what is he doing back there with no permission?" He responded by asking what did it matter and if I was going to open the house. I told him no, not until I saw some identification, which I would be sending to my office and my assistant down at the end of the driveway.

He more forcefully demanded, "Open the door!"

I said, "No, I won't, and your opportunity to see the property is over."

He started to swear at me, but I can make a long-shoreman blush, so I swore right back at him. Then he left, saying he was going to report me to the board. I replied, "Let me help you with that number."

After he left, I just sat and cried. I was firmly convinced I had overreacted and blown an opportunity for a sale. I went back to my office, and as I was walking in, my assistant was screaming for me. On the MLS was a note: blue van, no windows, New York plates just raped a real estate agent in a nearby town. I had just dodged a bullet, and it shook me to my core.

I love what I do, but I don't want to die doing it. This book is a comprehensive collection of self-help tools to create awareness and help us protect ourselves. I want to thank Kelly for providing her readers with amazing insight into the black soul of the predators who purposefully seek us out because we are vulnerable when we do our jobs.

Adorna Occhialini Carroll, DSA

79th Recipient of National Association of REALTORS®
Distinguished Service Award
ABR—Accredited Buyer Representative
SRS—Seller Representative Specialist
CRB—Certified RE Brokerage Manager
C-RETS—Certified RE Team Specialist
RENE—Real Estate Negotiation Expert
GRI—Graduate RE Institute

Real Estate Broker, REALTOR® Licensed in CT—REB 0752075
Real Estate Broker Licensed in
Massachusetts—1000406-RE-RB
President, Referrals Only CT, LLC—REB 0790419—
ReferralsOnlyCT.com
President Dynamic Directions, Inc.—DynamicDirections.com
Convention Speaker, Advanced Skill Trainer and Association
Management Consultant
Partner, CAC Business Consultants

f *Facebook.com/AdornaSpeaks*
in *Linkedin—AdornaCarroll*
○ *Twitter—@AdornaCarroll*
✉ *Adorna@Adorna.com*

chapter one

THE TRAGEDY THAT CHANGED MY TRAJECTORY

I t was September 25, 2014. I had just finished dinner with my family when the news broke. A real estate agent in central Arkansas had a promising showing with new clients, but was now missing. As news agencies raced to the scene to cover the breaking story, I caught a glimpse of the missing agent's family in front of the home she had been showing. It was wrapped in yellow caution tape.

Standing frozen in front of the television, my feet felt like they were encased in solid ice. I couldn't believe what I was hearing. In disbelief, my heart sank further as I watched the news story unfold of this family living an unimaginable nightmare. With my heart in the pit of my stomach I thought: *This could be any one of us at any time.* A distraught son was looking for his mom; a husband who would later become a suspect was searching for his wife, and the police themselves were just beginning to try to put the puzzle pieces together. Her car was still sitting in the driveway where she parked for the showing, but there was no sign of her.

Where was Beverly Carter? News reporters continued to gather information. Even though I was several states away, it was breaking news where I lived. The reporters stayed on the scene waiting for any information to share through the many days that followed this tragic event. The television news showed Beverly Carter's friends and family lining the streets with missing person posters in hand, stopping traffic, and asking anyone and everyone if they had seen anything at all. Volunteers handed out fliers for businesses to post in windows. There was a palpable feeling of both desperation and hope as the family searched in what was undoubtedly the darkest moment of their lives.

Soon, real estate professionals from other states arrived to join the search in the hope of finding Beverly Carter. They set out in a massive grid, worked in numbered groups, walked through snake-infested swamps and murky soybean fields. They wore red t-shirts that read *#FindBeverly* and held candlelight vigils when it got too dark to continue with the search. For five days, I stayed glued to the news, unable to fathom the horror the Carter family was going through. On September 30, 2014, the news came that none of us wanted to hear. They had recovered Beverly Carter's body from a shallow grave.

A breaking news report showed area detectives standing at a podium in front of the police station alerting the public that a suspect was in custody, and we caught our first glimpse of the predator. Later we would learn about a second suspect, Mrs. Predator. Yes, his wife.

These murderers will not gain any sort of recognition here, and therefore, they will remain unnamed. This is not their story; it is Beverly's and her family's story that I share with you.

HOW DID IT HAPPEN?

After the police interrogation and formal arrest, and in the midst of the transfer to jail, reporters scrambled to get a comment from the predator who took Beverly's life. One reporter repeatedly asked, "Why Beverly? *Why Beverly!*" The formally charged suspect, with hands cuffed behind his back, seated in the back of a police car spoke right into the mic: "Because she was a rich broker who worked alone."

Now, I didn't personally know Beverly or her family, but I didn't need to. As a real estate professional myself, I understood that an attack on a fellow agent was an attack on all of us!

What we learned from the trial, court documents, and later from Beverly's son himself was that Beverly had been working with these new buyers for a while. Although she never met them in person, she had conversed with them several times by telephone, email, and text. Their phone numbers matched that of an out-of-state buyer. They used fictitious names with emails to match those names. The story they told Beverly was that they were relocating due to work, and they were cash buyers. As Beverly learned more about this couple and how to better serve them, she went out of her way to line up the right properties.

At office meetings, she spoke about these buyers,

filling in her co-workers with details of what they were looking for. She asked her peers to keep their ears and eyes open for anything coming on the market that might match what this couple was looking for.

Beverly also spoke of these buyers with her family while at home. As the consummate real estate professional, she was excited to help them with their real estate needs.

What Beverly didn't know was that this couple were not who they said they were. The husband was a seven-time felon. He never had any intention of purchasing a home, and he wasn't from out of state—in fact, he lived nearby. He and his wife had specifically targeted Beverly.

After many weeks of communication, these supposed buyers called Beverly and asked to see a specific property she knew was vacant, in poor shape, and probably not what they were looking for. This request must have raised a red flag for Beverly because she did something at that moment she reportedly had never done before. She made up a company policy on her own and stated, "I'm sorry, our company policy prohibits us from meeting alone in a rural area." What she didn't anticipate is that the wife would jump on the phone to say, "Hey! I'll be there too! Would your company be okay if it was the three of us there during this showing?"

Upon hearing this, Beverly may have felt a little safer with the wife being at the showing. She agreed to show them the home and set the meeting for 6 p.m.— before dark, because this particular property didn't have the utilities turned on.

The day of the showing began like most real estate agents' days do. Beverly attended a Continuing Education class followed by an Affiliate luncheon, where she won a gift card. She called home to her husband to let him know she would be picking up dinner. But first, she had to show that specific property to the new buyers. Her husband knew the house she was showing. It was just three doors down from where the pastor of their church lived. Although the home needed repairs, it was a lakefront home in a community where residents felt safe. They were even known to leave cars and doors unlocked.

Beverly arrived early to the showing, parked in the driveway, and continued to make calls and work from her car until the out-of-town clients arrived. Shortly thereafter, a little black vehicle pulled into the driveway, and Mr. Buyer exited the car, but Mrs. Buyer was not with him. This was not what they agreed to.

Mr. Buyer approached Beverly with a quick excuse, "I'm sorry, my wife got held up at work and can't join us." As soon as those lies stumbled from his lips, Beverly started receiving text messages from the wife apologizing for being held up at work. They asked Beverly to proceed with showing the property that day. While she toured the home with Mr. Buyer, he asked if she would take pictures and text them to his wife. In that way, according to Mrs. Buyer, it would be just as if she were on the showing with them.

Still eager to service her clients, Beverly agreed to show Mr. Buyer the home, sending photos and engaging by text with his wife. Beverly's son, Carl Carter Jr., would later comment on how those photos were so hard to see at the conclusion of the trial when the family finally received Beverly's cell phone back. The last ten photos on her camera roll were of the interior of the home she was showing. The very last photo exhibited motion blur, leaving behind a chilling detail that would later be revealed by the predator himself.

When Beverly and Mr. Buyer entered the second-floor bedroom, Beverly had just snapped a photo of the room to send to his wife. As she turned to exit the room, she was met with a taser on her side and a roll of duct tape. Her attacker would later proudly self-report that the last words he said to Beverly were, "You're about to have a very bad day."

After he tasered Beverly, he tied her hands behind her back, taped her ankles together, then wrapped the tape entirely around her head, over her eyes, and again over her mouth. Mr. Buyer then went outside and got in his car, backed it up to the front door, and placed Beverly in the trunk. Before he closed the trunk, he snapped a photo of Beverly and sent it to his wife to alert her that their plan was in motion.

What was the plan? Ransom money! These criminals chose Beverly based on her perceived wealth.

As a professional real estate agent, Beverly was over-joyed to help so many families realize their dreams of homeownership. She was proud of her accomplishments, so she marketed herself as the top producer she was. Many successful real estate agents do the same thing. What she didn't realize was that the same marketing would catch the attention of a predator.

Apparently, these predators never watched a ransom movie before to know that they don't end in the villain's favor. Their absurd plan was to demand a ransom for her safe return, and once it was received, they would never have to work again. Their big plan was to have Beverly's family push ransom money through to her credit cards and debit card. After placing Beverly in the trunk of his car, the predator took Beverly to a remote location and made her record the very first of what was supposed to be a series of ransom demands. He then took Beverly to his home and locked her up in the bathroom.

It was at that point that Mr. and Mrs. Buyer talked through their original plan. Beverly's family would never receive a ransom demand because Beverly did something she always did as a safety precaution: she did not take her purse inside to a showing. She left it in the front seat of her car, along with a file and a paper trail she created for all her clients. In the predator's haste to kidnap Beverly, he didn't even think about her purse. Realizing his mistake, he decided to go back to the vacant house to retrieve it while his armed wife stayed at their home and kept guard with her back against the bathroom door.

As the predator drove down the long, dark road to the property where he kidnapped Beverly, he discovered her family there—along with the flashing lights of police cars. When the family and law enforcement noticed his car approaching, the predator was stopped and questioned, then *allowed to leave!*

Immediately afterward, Beverly's husband's phone started to receive text messages from Beverly's phone. The first text message read, "Sorry phone was dead." The family felt immediate relief, but only temporarily because the next text message read, "Out having drinks with the girls." Beverly was not a drinker, and the family knew right away it was not her texting them.

With the predators' plans foiled, they did what most felons do when they see police cars with flashing lights—they panicked. Realizing their plan wouldn't work, they feared Beverly could identify the man and recall the woman's name from prescription bottles in the bathroom where she was being held. They decided to end Beverly's life.

They took everything of value from her, including the shirt she was wearing, which was later found hanging in the wife's closet. They completely wrapped her head and face in green duct tape. Then, to make sure she couldn't breathe, they cut several six-inch pieces of tape and continued to pile it over her face. They took her to a concrete plant where the husband once worked, and the wife held a flashlight while he dug a shallow grave. They then buried Beverly's body while her family searched for her.

Sadly, it was through a post on Facebook that Beverly's family would first learn that her body had been found. The predators were eventually caught. The husband lied his way through the court system and twisted his story into ugly and untrue accusations in an attempt to tarnish Beverly's reputation. He tried to make it seem like she was partially at fault, hurting her family even more deeply.

In the end, justice was finally handed down. The husband was sentenced to life in prison with no possibility of parole. His wife entered a plea deal, turned state's evidence, and received a 30-year prison sentence.

ADVOCATING FOR SAFETY

In the aftermath of this tragedy, Carl Carter Jr. realized just how important of an issue safety is for the real estate industry and made the decision that he would take action to help ensure a tragedy like his mother's murder would never happen again. As a result, Carl founded a nonprofit in Beverly's name that exists solely for safety awareness and victim advocacy training for the real estate industry, the Beverly Carter Foundation. (BeverlyCarterFoundation.org)

It was through Carl's advocacy for safety awareness that I eventually met the same young man I saw on television during that harrowing time. I was at our annual National Association of REALTORS® convention and attended something I wouldn't normally attend—a cocktail event. (Like Beverly, I don't drink.) I was standing at a table when Carl Carter Jr. walked in. He headed toward my table and, with his never-ending smile, just like his momma's, he started to introduce himself.

I stopped him and said, "I know exactly who you are." I explained to him that I had shared in the grief he and his family endured during that horrible nightmare. I further explained to him that immediately following that tragedy, I began to ask fellow real estate agents what their plans were for their personal safety.

He then reached into his pocket and pulled out his mom's name badge and showed it to me. As he held it up so I could see it, he explained to me that new buyers had purchased the home where the predators once lived and where Beverly was held captive. As the new owners were cleaning under the stove, they found Beverly's name badge split in half. Carl said it was a reminder not only of his mom, but also of the careless disregard these people had for Beverly's life. Like her name badge, they so easily discarded Beverly's life, too.

LEVERAGING TRAGEDY FOR CHANGE

Witnessing Beverly's family go through the anguish no family should ever have to endure really hit a nerve with me. I've been showing and selling real estate, conducting open houses, and working with strangers for over two decades. Although I always felt like I was being careful, I began to realize some of the dangerous safety mistakes I was making along the way. I, too, marketed myself as a top producer. I, too, showed vacant homes to strangers. I, too, felt safer with a wife at a showing.

In an industry where it takes thirty to sixty days (sometimes longer) to earn a paycheck, I know where we real estate agents put our focus. Our success, our livelihood, and that of our family depend on how many sales we make.

I get it, and if you are a real estate agent, I bet you do, too. But real estate is one of the last industries that still makes house calls, and our livelihood is dependent on each of us being able to conduct our work safely. Ask any of our loved ones what is most important to them, and they will tell you it is for us to return home safely at the end of the workday.

I decided a very long time ago that I wouldn't stand by and be a target when there were precautions I could take to protect my safety. I knew even then that I wouldn't allow my fellow agents to become targets either! Carl Carter Jr. and others with the Beverly Carter Foundation travel the nation to educate agents on personal safety while at work. Every time this young man tells this horrific story to complete strangers in an effort to save just one life, he is forced to relive the tragedy of the kidnapping and murder of his mom. Yet he does it with such grace, honoring Beverly and her dedication to the profession.

With the help of my local association, I would later bring Carl Carter Jr. to my hometown so he could share the story of Beverly Carter with agents from my area. I kept in touch with the Beverly Carter Foundation through the years, sharing their mission and messaging of agent safety anywhere and everywhere I could. I was overjoyed to hear from Carl again in a personal email.

"Hi, Kelly! I hope this email finds you well," it read. "I have a little something I'd like to mail you in appreciation of all your efforts in agent safety. Happy Thanksgiving to you!—Carl"

Not only did I receive a photo of his momma with her big, beautiful smile, but he also sent me a journal. It was in that journal that I began the journey of writing this book for you.

Throughout the course of my career, I've been blessed with leadership positions that have afforded me the opportunity to have a direct connection with other real estate professionals and speak to their safety. As a special guest on the *OPRAH* show, I have educated consumers around the world on predatory practices and spoken to their safety. In the years that followed the murder of Beverly Carter, I underwent intensive safety training, studying dangerous personalities and predators under some of the world's most influential mentors and trainers. I had the privilege to learn from FBI, ATF, CIA, Department of Defense certified military interrogators, and Naval Human Intelligence Officers. They worked on high-profile cases like 9/11, Guantanamo Bay, and the JonBenet Ramsey murder.

I became a Master Certified Body Language expert. I have taught the body language of predators to real estate agents in London, Canada, Romania, and other countries across the globe. I also studied with a US Marshall about how to analyze deceptive statements and conversations, a skill that is particularly useful for someone in my line of work.

While the real estate industry is full of opportunities, it is also an industry in a safety crisis. As real estate agents, we have a lot of safety tips and tools at our disposal. These are all great—anything that gets you thinking about your personal safety is a big *win*! But the reality is often we read them, or read past them, and move on. Unfortunately, most of the advice is reactive, focusing on what to do while a crime is possibly already occurring.

This book is different. My aim is to not only open your eyes to the dangerous personalities around us, but also arm you with Mastery skills and teach you how to identify and protect yourself from those that mean you harm. My focus is on how you can proactively avoid becoming a victim in the first place!

Upon a successful home closing, I always thank my clients for allowing me to be part of their journey in finding their way to a new home. I would like to invite you now on a journey that also helps you to find your way home each and every day—safely.

chapter two

A SERIOUS PROBLEM

Most people wouldn't think of real estate as a dangerous profession. Yet the United States Department of Labor has listed real estate sales and leasing as a hazardous occupation. In one recent year, they recorded eighty-seven deaths.[1] That doesn't take into consideration other crimes committed against real estate agents, such as robberies, physical assaults, or sexual crimes. And there are many crimes that go unreported as a result of a victim's fear or sense of embarrassment.

> Real estate professionals put themselves at risk every day—not on purpose, nor even accidentally. We assume the inherent risks while fulfilling our everyday job requirements.

Take a moment right now and search the words *Real Estate Agent Attack* with your internet browser. Sadly, the horror stories you'll see listed in the results are real. All of the professionals in the stories you'll see were innocent victims. Predatory crimes against real estate professionals are a growing problem. Real estate professionals put themselves at risk every day—not on purpose, nor even accidentally. We assume the inherent risks while fulfilling our everyday job requirements.

CAN YOU RECOGNIZE A PREDATOR?

Criminals come in all shapes and sizes. If I asked you to imagine what a predator looks like, what would you see? Is your predator male or female? If he's male, is he clean-shaven or bearded? Is your predator covered in tattoos and piercings? How is he or she dressed? What about the size of your predator—short or tall? Young or older?

> Predators don't fit a specific image; they are like chameleons and blend into the community and circumstance as if they belong there.

We each have a unique preconceived idea of what a predator looks like, but I ask you, how accurate is that picture in your mind? Would you be able to tell if your next potential client is a prospect or a predator by the way they look, sound, or their supposed intent? Far too often, the answer is no.

Ted Bundy was a young law student who dressed professionally. Most women thought of him as charming, intelligent, and good-looking. Yet he raped, kidnapped, and murdered approximately 30 girls and women.

Similarly, no one would have imagined a clean-cut second-year medical student would answer a Craigslist ad for massage services, meet up with the masseuse, attempt to rob her, and ultimately murder her. He was dubbed the Craigslist Killer.

Or how about the little 67-year-old lady who ran a

boarding house in Sacramento, California, and murdered some of her elderly and mentally disabled renters before cashing their Social Security checks? She was convicted of nine confirmed murders, with six more unconfirmed.

Predators don't fit a specific image; they are like chameleons and blend into the community and circumstance as if they belong there. And they don't always act alone. After several face-to-face meetings with a couple of new clients who were supposedly getting married, a female real estate agent from Durham, North Carolina went to the man's home to finalize the listing. While there, she was beaten and almost raped. She would later learn that the couple had planned the attack together after picking her out of a real estate magazine.

And let's not forget the husband-and-wife team that kidnapped and murdered Beverly Carter and shook this industry to its core, creating an open wound to our collective sense of safety that still exists today.

PREDATORS DON'T DISCRIMINATE

No one—male or female—is immune to being victimized by a criminal. According to one affidavit, a male real estate agent in Nashville, Tennessee was bent over trying to open a lockbox at a property when he was confronted by a gunman who reportedly said to him, "I'll shoot you! I'll [expletive] kill you!" The gunman told him to start running, so the agent threw his keys and phone into the bushes and took off. He hid behind some parked vehicles as he witnessed his own vehicle being stolen by the gunman.

A Milwaukee, Wisconsin male real estate agent was

attacked while showing a rental property. A woman called him as a potential renter, and upon meeting her at the door and entering the home, he was ambushed. Two masked men came out of separate bedrooms and pistol-whipped him. All of this happened while his wife waited in the car for him to finish showing the unit.

Maybe you believe there is always safety in numbers? In Huntington Beach, California, police announced that a home inspector was killed, and two agents shot while on a property visit. In this case, family members were having a dispute over the sale of the home and violence broke out. The real estate professionals were not the targets, but they were the victims.

A 26-year-old female real estate agent in Columbus, Ohio, had been working with a male buyer for quite some time. Over the course of working with the agent, the supposed buyer met her several times in her office and developed a rapport with her. He said he was a nuclear physicist from Tennessee and wanted a high-end property that he would be paying cash for.

Later, the buyer called the agent to view a property. Before she left the office, she asked a veteran agent to join her. The buyer met both agents at the house but managed to separate them during the showing. He then used a stun gun to attack the young agent. She was able to scream and began to fight off her attacker. As she screamed, it alerted the other agent and caused the attacker to flee.

The agents were able to get the predator's license plate number and phoned the police. The so-called nuclear physicist from Tennessee ended up being a local commercial cleaning serviceman and a convicted rapist.

When he was caught, his vehicle was searched by police, and they found MLS information with the young agent's picture circled in ink.

In Westchester, California the body of a 45-year-old real estate agent and father of five was found inside a bank-owned home listed for more than half a million dollars. His family had been posting missing person fliers around town after he failed to return home from work four days prior. An agent preparing to show the home notified police when she found the open lockbox with the keys missing. He was stabbed multiple times.

A Canadian predator spent months plotting the kidnapping of a well-known local businessman. He posed as a buyer and contacted a real estate agent under the guise of purchasing the businessman's mansion for $2.38 Million.

Along with seven accomplices, he kidnapped both the businessman and the real estate agent when they went to an upstairs room in the home to finalize the deal. According to court documents, after a week of being held captive with his hands and feet locked in chains, the real estate agent died of a heart attack. His body was placed in two garbage bags and buried. He was found six months later.

A 71-year-old Wisconsin real estate agent and grandmother of sixteen was showing a home when her client choked her with her own scarf and began beating her with a fireplace poker after she said something he didn't like—the price of the home! In his confession, the murderer and registered sex offender, who had served ten years in prison for the attempted rape and stabbing of a woman prior to this attack, stated he then set the house on fire to cover up the evidence after he noticed she was moving and still conscious. An autopsy revealed that the agent died of smoke inhalation. Deputies were able to track her down when her family reported that she didn't make it home, and her husband asked them to check the address of her last known showing.

One New York real estate agent, in an effort to get a listing, hurried to a home that turned out to be occupied by a paroled convict. Within minutes of the agent arriving at his home, he slit her throat.

A male real estate agent from Maryland was working out of a model home in what was generally assumed to be a safe residential development when he was attacked. He managed to call 911, but the dispatcher could only hear what sounded to be like heavy breathing followed by someone repeatedly shouting, "Where is the money?" When police arrived, they discovered the agent had been shot and killed.

A Connecticut agent felt something was wrong when she went on a listing appointment and the homeowner kept asking her if she wanted something to drink and if she'd like to see the attic. She was sitting in the living room and happened to look over the side of the chair where she saw a local real estate magazine with pictures of real estate agents circled in red. When the homeowner excused himself to go to the bathroom, she was able to escape.

An agent in Los Angeles who had just earned his real estate license was shot and fatally wounded while canvassing a neighborhood for clients in an effort to make his first sale before Christmas.

And it is not only new clients with whom we need to

be cautious. When one Michigan real estate agent went into the conference room in his office to meet with a former client, he was shot and killed at point-blank range. His prior client believed he paid too much for his home after property values declined. Instead of blaming the current market, he put the blame on the agent.

IT'S TIME FOR A CULTURE OF SAFETY

Most safety experts agree that as long as we continue to work alone with the random public showing and selling homes, we are at risk and remain vulnerable. Showing and selling homes is how we make a living. That is literally the nature of our business! Yet, criminals see us as easy prey, and they use that very necessary way we conduct business against us.

> Most safety experts agree that as long as we continue to work alone with the random public showing and selling homes, we are at risk and remain vulnerable.

To function at the bare minimum in this career, a real estate agent must take calculated risks every single day just to perform their duties. And because this business can be competitive, the desire to make a sale can lead to short-cutting safety procedures.

The National Association of REALTORS® (NAR) recognized a safety program was needed to educate REALTORS® about the potential safety risks and dangers they face on the job.

To better understand the scope of the safety risks before us, NAR's research department conducts an annual survey of members. According to the 2020

Member Safety Report, 23% of the survey respondents experienced a situation that made them fear for their safety.[2] Two specific areas highlighted were open houses and showings, with 31% of respondents reporting they felt unsafe during an open house and 31% felt unsafe during a showing. 5% of REALTORS® reported that they have been a victim of a crime.

NAR's REALTOR® Safety program helps members reduce risk and manage situations they may face through knowledge, awareness, and empowerment. Safety tips, tools, and resources for REALTORS®, state and local associations, and brokerages can be found by visiting NAR. realtor/safety.

Since 2003, NAR has designated September as REALTOR® safety month, but real estate agents are vulnerable to attacks from thieves, sexual predators, and murderers all year long. All it takes is one showing, one client, one open house—just one time for you to come face to face with your safety being at risk.

Does your brokerage/company offer a safety program to educate you on the risks involved while on the job, and do they have resources available to help keep you safe? An Orange County, California real estate office was the scene of a mass shooting where four people were killed, including a nine-year-old boy who died in his mother's arms. The shooter was believed to have had both a business and personal relationship with the victims.

In Watertown, New York, a brokerage lost both of its owners in a deadly shooting involving one of its own agents.

The Pinellas County, Florida Sheriff's office stated a

man was angry that his longtime girlfriend was laid off from her job where she worked as an office manager for a real estate office. The man shot and killed a broker at the office, wounded another agent, and then killed himself.

Brokerages are not immune to civil lawsuits, especially when something happens to one of their agents. Establishing a safety program in your office is one of the most effective ways to protect your most valuable assets: your agents. Just one incident can cause significant disruption and cost to you, as well as the agents and their families. It can also damage workplace morale, productivity, turnover—and cost you your reputation. Brokerages can not only help keep their agents safe, but also significantly reduce their liability by adopting, implementing, and supporting safety policies and procedures company-wide, documenting every step of the way.

> Brokerages are also not immune to civil lawsuits, especially when something happens with one of their agents.

The accompaniment to this book, *Mastery Skills of Safe Practices for Real Estate Professionals,* was built to meet that need and is the perfect place to start. Simply by supplying new and existing agents with this companion, brokerages can begin to document an agent's acknowledgment of the various risks in the industry, and more importantly the safety practices available to them.

Additionally, the *Real Estate Agent Safety Discussion Form* allows brokerages to document which safety discussions were held, when safety discussions were held, who facilitated that discussion, and a roster of everyone in attendance for that safety discussion.

Remember, there is no commission more valuable than your life. Take charge of your safety now. Don't leave it up to anyone else.

The Mastery Skills highlighted throughout this book are designed so that they can also be adopted and introduced at office meetings, providing safety training all year long.

No one plans to be in a dangerous situation, and no one can guarantee your personal safety. We all need to be prepared for any possibility, and we can certainly reduce the chances of having dangerous encounters with an intentional approach to our personal safety.

Remember, there is no commission more valuable than your life. Take charge of your safety now. Don't leave it up to anyone else. With an intentional approach to personal safety, you greatly minimize your chance of becoming the next victim.

chapter three

A RISKY BUSINESS?

A fifteen-year real estate veteran received a floor call while at the office in North Carolina one morning. A man identifying himself as James was calling, saying he wanted to purchase all the waterfront property in one particular subdivision in the area. Because it was highly unusual that someone would want to purchase *all* of the waterfront property in a subdivision, the agent explained to him that he would need to make an appointment and meet her in the office to review his needs.

She set the appointment for 3:30 that afternoon, only half believing James would actually show. But at 3:30, a young man who came across as assertive and matter-of-fact arrived. The agent led him back to the glass-enclosed conference room: "Hello, James, it's nice to meet you," the agent said.

"I'm not James," he replied. "James is who I work for." The agent sensed something was off but couldn't exactly pinpoint what it was. She continued to dig deeper as to why this young man was interested in so much waterfront property. He explained that he worked for a company that had been very successful at setting up Airbnb rentals up and down the East Coast and was looking for more opportunities.

Over the course of an hour or more, the agent worked to identify property that might work for this buyer, enlisting the assistance of several other agents in the office to look through plat books and research neighborhood covenants for different areas.

During this time, the young man let the agent know that he had made his company $25 million as he had been on the road for the last three years. When she asked him where he was from, he answered, "I don't have an address at the moment; I've been on the road." She pressed him with, "Well, everyone is from somewhere; where are you from?" He answered, "Detroit."

The agent brought up a couple of properties for sale that would be aligned with what he said he was looking for. One of those properties happened to be a currently vacant home that her father-in-law had built which the agent and her husband had just renovated and put up for sale. When she offered to show the home to the buyer, he agreed.

As they were leaving the office, the agent stopped at the front desk to let the receptionist know she was going out to show that address. At that time, she asked the buyer for his business card. He replied that he had left them in his car. The agent then stated, "That's okay. When we get to the house, you can give it to me there."

As a practice, this real estate agent did not let clients ride with her in her vehicle, mainly for insurance reasons. She told the buyer that he would have to follow her to the showing. When he pulled out to follow her, the agent noticed he was in an old car with a handicap placard hanging from the mirror. It didn't fit the profile of a young, healthy man, traveling up and down the East coast for three years, making his company $25 million.

While en route, the agent called her husband and let him know she was headed to show that address. She also mentioned what she noticed about the buyer's car and how the picture that he painted of himself did not match up. Still, she told her husband it would probably be okay. Her husband asked if she wanted him to join her at the showing. She said, "No, I have the home next door listed for sale as well and those owners are home; I've got this."

When they arrived at the vacant home, the agent opened the door, and she immediately sensed danger. The buyer insisted she go in first, but she was careful to follow behind him. Because of her feeling that something wasn't right, she was reluctant to close the front door.

The buyer stood in the entryway like a statue and didn't move. So the agent tried to get him moving: "If you go forward, you're going to be in the dining room, and if you go right, you're going to be in the family room. You choose which way to go."

He pointed and asked, "What is that room over there?"

"Bedroom number one," the agent replied. As she went into the bedroom ahead of him to flip on the light switch, the hair on the back of her neck stood up when she realized she could be trapped in that room with him if he decided to shut the door. She'd never experienced that feeling before in her fifteen years of showing homes.

Quickly she started backtracking her steps, being

careful not to get trapped in the room. She made her way to a Jack-and-Jill bathroom and then into another bedroom that had access to a screened-in porch with a door to the outside.

As soon as they were in the bedroom, the buyer grabbed her arm and said, "I'm not who I said I am." She knew at that point that she had to either fight or get out.

Pulling her arm back, she said, "What do you mean? Who are you?"

"I'm a porn star," he replied, "and you would look really good on camera." The agent immediately ran to the glass sliding doors at the screened porch, but he jumped in front of the doors and laughingly asked, "Where do you think you're going?" He grabbed her again and began to batter her with sexual questions. She knew if she didn't get out that door, he was going to rape her, beat her, or worse.

The agent still cannot recall how she managed to get through the sliding doors onto the screened porch, but she did. The predator then jumped in front of the door which led from the porch into the yard. The agent fought for her life to get out that door, too. When she finally did, he ran after her.

She ran to the neighbor's home, the one she had listed, and was able to call 911. The predator was apprehended the following day. It turned out he was actually an in-town, 20-year-old aviation college student. He was charged with kidnapping and assault, served four months in prison, and was released on probation for two years with an ankle bracelet.

The agent now speaks out, sharing her story with others in the industry, hoping to make a difference in the lives of fellow agents. She no longer shows homes by herself.

RISKS AND REWARDS

A career in real estate can be extremely rewarding. In fact, most real estate professionals including myself will tell you that it is more than just a career; it's a *passion* and a *lifestyle*. With a wide range of career options and many possible career tracks to follow, real estate professionals are able to add a specialty path or two to expand their career even further. For ambitious, hard-working professionals, a career in real estate offers flexibility and significant income opportunities not easily found elsewhere.

> A career in real estate can be extremely rewarding. In fact, most real estate professionals including myself will tell you that it is more than just a career; it's a *passion* and a *lifestyle*.

Real Estate, renting, and leasing constitute the largest sector of the United States' economy accounting for 13% of the national GDP.[1] One of the most universal signs of success and prosperity is homeownership, and a real estate agent is at the center of making it happen, opening doors of opportunity for the clients they work with and the communities they serve. Every real estate agent knows how rewarding that is—both financially and emotionally.

Yet real estate is an industry that can be fraught with risk, especially if agents are blind to—or knowingly disregard—basic safety precautions. Just one single case of violence can seriously affect the victim, other agents, brokerage and community.

Granted, safety is not only a real estate industry concern. Violence in the workplace is a burning issue across several industries.

According to the Federal Bureau of Investigations 2020 Annual Crime Statistics Report, a violent crime in the United States occurs every 24.7 seconds—and that is just the crime known to law enforcement. Many more go unreported.[2]

2020 CRIME CLOCK STATISTICS

A Violent Crime Occurred Every	24.7 seconds
One Murder every	24.4 minutes
One Rape every	4.2 minutes
One Robbery every	2.2 minutes
One Aggrevated Assault every	34.3 seconds
A property Crime occured every	4.9 second
One Burglary every	4.9 seconds
One Larceny-theft every	30.5 seconds
One Motor Vehicle Theft every	6.9 seconds

We hear about workplace shootings all too often. We even worry about sending our children to school, a place we all used to think of as a safety zone. The unfortunate reality is our personal safety can be at risk every day, no matter what business we are in or what activity we are engaged in.

Agent safety is not a comfortable topic; it is rarely discussed, and is not necessarily well-received. For some real estate agents, the pressure to get a client and make a sale supersedes following recommended safety practices because they think it might cause friction and slow down the process. We live in a day and age where part of providing a great customer experience involves meeting their demands and expectations for speed and efficiency.

> For some real estate agents, the pressure to get a client and make a sale supersedes following recommended safety practices because they think it might cause friction and slow down the process.

But I can attest that it *is* possible to have safety awareness first and foremost in our daily routine, building personal safety right into our business as a natural habit while still addressing clients' and customers' acute needs. Working with care, creative thinking, and employing the same safety process every single time with every single client will allow you to keep your safety at the forefront of your business and remain competitive without slowing down the process.

MORE THAN A CHECKLIST

Although safety in the real estate industry has evolved over the years, we're still not where we need to be. Yes, we have all seen the endless checklists of agent safety tips, tricks, and resources. If you do a quick internet search for "real estate safety tips", you'll find dozens of results with the same basic information repeated again and again.

There is nothing wrong with these sites sharing safety tips—it at least brings awareness to the issue—but do these checklists work? Given the fact that agents are still being attacked at an alarming rate, it's worth questioning.

Let's take a quick look at some of the tips included on many of the safety checklists:

CHECKLIST TIP

Always let someone know where you are going.

Reality Check: A 30-year-old Decatur, IL agent had plans to meet up with her family at a local festival. She had told her family that she was meeting prospective buyers at a particular vacant home right before the fair and then would join the family afterward. However, when she didn't show and repeated calls to her phone went unanswered, her family notified the police.

When police went to check on her at the home, they found her deceased on the kitchen floor. She had been strangled and beaten. Next to her was her daily agenda that she was carrying. It had the date, time, and (fake)names of the buyers she was supposed to meet at that home that day. Her case remains unsolved.

CHECKLIST TIP

Always meet new clients at the office first.

Reality Check: A young man interested in seeing single-family upscale homes wasn't much different than any of her other clients at the time, according to a St. Petersburg, Florida real estate agent. He was well-groomed, soft spoken, and very confident, even when meeting other agents at her office. He told her he was a DEA agent who was relocating to the area from Naples.

After spending several hours together viewing homes around St. Petersburg, the man requested to go back to a home they already viewed for a second showing. That is when he attacked.

They went to measure a wall, and she turned her back on him. She let her guard down. She reported that she felt him take two, hard quick steps behind her. Then he hit her in the head with a gun and she went down hard. She knew instantly what had happened. He hit her so hard, she saw stars and came right out of her shoes. She was sure she would be raped, robbed, or murdered.[3]

He then held a knife to her throat and threatened her not to move. He used cable ties to restrain her, shattering her elbow in the process. He stole her jewelry and her purse and demanded her ATM password before shoving her into a closet. After several attempts, she was finally able to break free, jump out a window, and run to a neighboring house. The predator was identified through video captured while he was accessing her account through the ATM. It took six long years before this agent would face her attacker in court. The predator was eventually sentenced to life in prison. The agent left her real estate career to work for an airline.[3]

CHECKLIST TIP

Never host an open house alone.

Reality Check: The bodies of two female sales agents, ages 21 and 33, were discovered in a model home during an open house event they had been conducting together.

A convicted felon, who was still on parole, entered the home and used a handgun to force them to undress and reveal the PINs for their debit cards. After calling the banks to learn the amount of their current balances, the predator choked both agents and shot them, using the open house balloons as a sound buffer.

When the builder, whose office was located in the model home's basement, heard the door chime of the security system indicating that someone had exited the sales office, he went upstairs to meet with the agents. There he discovered one body and called 911. The responding police officer discovered the second body. The predator was later apprehended, found guilty of malice murder, and sentenced to death.

CHECKLIST TIP

Always show homes before dark.

Reality Check: In many parts of the country, that is a difficult task to follow for approximately five months of the year. The reality is that danger doesn't just lurk in the dark; the crimes you have read about in this chapter all happened within daylight business hours.

CHECKLIST TIP

Have a safety app on your phone.

Reality Check: Most safety apps require the user to have their phone in hand, app open, good reception, and be able to type in some information. Assuming that violence is already being committed against us, why wouldn't we just dial 911 if we actually did have our cell phones in our hands and had the ability to make a call or open an app?

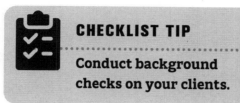

CHECKLIST TIP

Conduct background checks on your clients.

Reality Check: A popular pre-screening app that allows agents to run instant background checks on prospective clients is being advertised as a safety tool resource.

Unfortunately, not all arrests and convictions make it into the criminal database. And it also assumes that prospective clients use their real names, which we have seen is certainly not always the case. This may provide the agent with a false sense of security.

Important to note: Running background checks can also pose legal issues. Agents are at risk of violating fair housing laws. The Department of Housing and Urban Development (HUD) released a statement indicating that "Criminal records-based barriers to housing are likely to have a disproportionate impact on minority home seekers. While having a criminal record is not a protected characteristic under the Fair Housing Act, criminal history-based restrictions on housing opportunities violate the Act if, without justification, their burden falls more often on renters or other housing market participants of one race or national origin over another."[4]

Attempts at improving agent safety have been largely ineffective through the years, mostly because we didn't comprehend the magnitude of what was before us. While some tips, tricks, apps, and resources available to real estate agents may have been helpful tools in your safety toolbox at that time, they fell short of being truly effective in victim prevention.

I have studied literally hundreds of crimes against real estate professionals, and several obvious issues surfaced:

1. Real estate agents often fail to focus on prevention. We are reactive rather than proactive when it comes to our safety, and that is a far more dangerous position to take.

2. We don't take responsibility for our own safety. Too many agents assume someone else—usually their broker or association—is protecting them, which is not the case.

3. Most of the crime committed against real estate agents could have been prevented if only the agent had a better understanding of the behavioral science of criminology, the prototype of criminals wishing us harm, the nature of the crimes most often committed against us, and how to conduct business in a safer manner.

In the following chapters, I will be addressing these issues and others in depth, so that by the end of this book, you will have a much greater understanding of how to protect yourself from becoming a crime statistic while conducting business efficiently and doing the job that you love.

chapter four

PREDATORS OR OPPORTUNISTS

I t was just before closing time on November 25, 2012, in the sales office of a real estate development in Lehigh County, Pennsylvania. An agent in the office was alone at the time when a man entered and asked for a tour of the model home. Because he did not ask any questions regarding the homes, pricing, or any of the typical buyer questions, her sixth sense told her not to go with him. Instead, she told him to go ahead and take a look by himself.

The man went into the model home and stayed there for approximately forty-five minutes. He then returned to the office and told the agent there was a water leak. He asked her to return with him to the model home so he could show her the leak, but she refused. A male co-worker of the agent then entered the office, at which point the buyer quickly left. He went to his pickup truck and waited for the agent's male co-worker to leave, but after a while, he apparently got tired of waiting and drove off.

When the two real estate agents went to check the property for the supposed leak, they found all the lights out, curtains drawn, and no evidence of any issues. They called the police, who soon located the man and executed search warrants of his pickup truck and his home. At his home, they found numerous realty brochures and the female real estate agent's business card.

During questioning, the man admitted to officers that he had faked interest in the home and tried to get the agent alone, choosing closing time for that reason. He planned to rape her and called his search for a victim his "full-time work." He spent five months working on his plan and had put together a list of hundreds of real estate agents. The list included their names, where they lived, places of employment and business address. In his own words:

> I did a massive on-line search of these people (realtors) . . . I had a plan of action. . . For three months, I drove around every Sunday. I used my truck-driving skills to map out my route. Once I lost my job, I really put myself into it. It was full-time work. I want to attack every girl I see, so I was drinking all the time. . . I had a profile. I wanted someone, one of them pretty looking Paris Hilton type thing. I had a very specific guideline. . . The urges were so compelling. I was fighting it with alcohol.[1]

He was arrested.

When police searched his truck, they found the "rape kit" he planned on using, consisting of two handguns with several rounds of ammunition, four knives, duct tape, a ski mask, gloves, metal chains with padlocks, and a rope. Police also found handwritten notes in the man's home and truck, including one that read, "If you are reading this, I found a realtor woman and raped her. I have been planning and have wanted this my whole life."

In another note police found, the man wrote, "I know it is wrong, but I cannot fight the urges. I truly enjoy the hunt and cannot wait for my prize." Yet another read, "I have been planning and wanted this my whole life, the help I need is too great, and I would rather die."

In his diary labeled "Open House", he also drew pictures about the rape. A suicide note left at his home included a statement that he planned on raping two other agents instead of the victim, but the other agents were accompanied by a number of people. He also wrote that he would kill himself after the rape by setting the model home on fire.

This predator's Facebook account, which was still active at the time of this writing, shows some alarming posts:

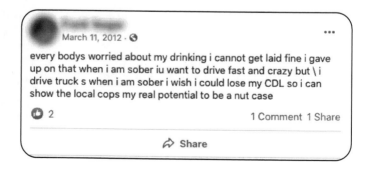

March 11, 2012 ·

every bodys worried about my drinking i cannot get laid fine i gave up on that when i am sober iu want to drive fast and crazy but \ i drive truck s when i am sober i wish i could lose my CDL so i can show the local cops my real potential to be a nut case

2   1 Comment 1 Share

Share

September 3, 2012 · Perkasie, PA · 🌐

I AM HELLS REALTOR

2 Shares

November 21, 2012 · Quakertown, PA · 🌐

OPEN HOUSE DECEMBER 21 ST BRIGHT AND EARLY LIVING SPACE IN HELL IS TIGHT BUY NOW BEFORE IT IS TO LATE REMEMBER HELLS REALTOR GREETS YOU

2 Comments

↗ Share

hahahaha

8y

this add is sponserd by colt // hollow points the expressway to the next world

8y

June 5, 2012 · Sellersville, PA · 🌐

got nothing that important to lose

👍 1   2 Comments

September 23, 2012 · Sellersville, PA · 🌐

fire is pure death is freedom i will be purified then liberated and will depart this world into a fiery hell

November 11, 2012 · Quakertown, PA · 🌐

if you are a realtor be happy i am shitfaced go sell some houses

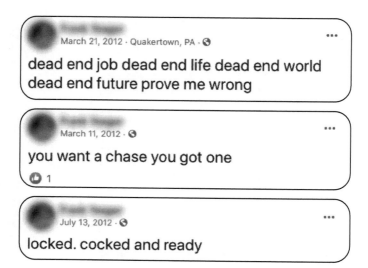

March 21, 2012 · Quakertown, PA

dead end job dead end life dead end world dead end future prove me wrong

March 11, 2012

you want a chase you got one

👍 1

July 13, 2012

locked. cocked and ready

The predator was convicted of attempted rape. He was sentenced to between ten and twenty years in federal prison. He later appealed his conviction, claiming his lawyer provided ineffective assistance by not contesting whether his confession was obtained legally. In June 2017, the Supreme Court upheld the ruling, citing the man as a "dangerous, full-blown psychopath." It's also important for all real estate agents to understand this predator may be released soon.

THE PREDATOR'S CRIME CYCLE

Violent, predatory crime is not random. Real estate agent attacks are primarily predatory crimes. Understanding a predator's crime cycle provides agents with an opportunity to prevent being selected as a target in predatory assaults.

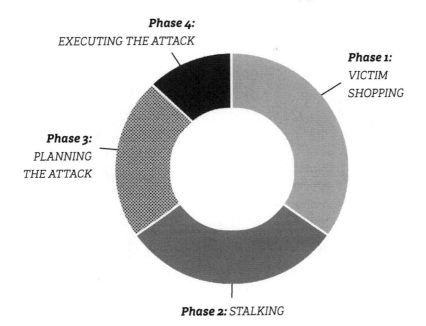

Phase 1: VICTIM SHOPPING. In this phase, a predator will shop for a victim and identify his or her target. Their choice is not a random one. The victim can be male or female. Although women are more likely to be chosen over men because they are generally perceived as weaker and more vulnerable, predatory crimes against male real estate agents are on the rise. Depending on the motive, the predator will seek out someone who meets their specific needs or will satisfy a desire.

Phase 2: STALKING. This is the predator's research and evaluation stage. Stalkers no longer need a physical presence to monitor and access the information they want to know. The internet gives them a powerful identity and allows them to become virtual stalkers and virtual predators.

While initially focusing on available professional information, a predator will soon move on to gathering personal information on their target, including their age, marital status, personal interests, home address, children's names and which schools they attend, frequented places like coffee shops or fitness gyms, etc. You get the idea! Search engines and social media are increasingly becoming tools that a predator will use to identify, study, and track their victim, making it much easier for them to get as much information as possible on the subject of their interest before physically stalking them.

> A predator wants to commit the perfect crime without getting caught, so at this stage, with a list of potential victims, the predator may not strike the first, second, or even tenth agent they target. But the assault *will* eventually occur.

Phase 3: PLANNING THE ATTACK.

The predator has entered a fantasy stage. This stage of pre-assault may run simultaneously with the personal information gathering stage and/or physically stalking the victim. The predator may be focusing on several agents simultaneously.

In this fantasy and planning stage, the predator is creating a time in life with you in it. A predator wants to commit the perfect crime without getting caught, so at this stage, with a list of potential victims, the predator may not strike the first, second, or even tenth agent they target. But an assault *will* eventually occur.

Phase 4: EXECUTING THE ATTACK. This may be your initial contact with the predator, and believe it or not, it typically starts with a phone call for a home showing. The predator may forego the call altogether and show up at the last minute to an open house or before closing the office. However, the goal remains the same, and that is to get you alone and isolated. Once the stage is set, power, position, speed, and surprise all feed into the fantasy of predatory attack.

CRIMES OF OPPORTUNITY

Upon hearing the news that a real estate agent has been attacked, most people automatically think that the agent was chosen at random and the attack was spontaneous. The majority of the time, however, that is not the case. Most of these attacks are predatory crimes rather than crimes of opportunity, and it is important to understand the difference.

A predatory criminal will take the time to carefully choose a victim, research and stalk the victim, and formulate a plan before ever meeting their victim. By contrast, crimes of opportunity are more similar to what is often called street crime, where an opportunist criminal may not be planning a crime at all but will act if an inviting opportunity arises. These types of crimes are very rare as far as attacks on real estate agents are concerned.

The following chart outlines behavioral differences between Predators and Opportunists in crimes committed against real estate agents.

PREDATORS	OPPORTUNISTS
CRIMES COMMITTED–Stalking, Violent Assault, Sexual Assault, Murder, Robbery	**CRIMES COMMITTED**–Burglary, Robbery – At times can escalate to Assault or Murder
MOTIVES–Power, Control, Satisfy a desire	**MOTIVES**–Drugs, Profit, Financial gain
GOALS–Isolate you, Gain control, Power, Manipulation and Intimidation, Death	**GOALS**–The criminal requires isolation and lurks in the background with hidden intentions.
EMOTION–No Conscience, No Empathy, No Remorse, Callous, Calculating, Has little fear of acting on intentions, Aggressive pleasure	**EMOTION**–Jealousy, Revenge, Anger, Fear of being caught
STRATEGY - Targeted–Follows a progression pattern to carefully select a target. Stalking–They enjoy enjoy the hunt and the element of surprise. Will take time to rehearse scenarios and form a plan. Does not give up easily or easily deterred.	**STRATEGY**–Random–Risk vs Return. The lower the risk of being caught and the higher of return, the greater the likelihood of theft. They make decisions quickly.

I have had the unique experience of meeting with Frank Abagnale Jr., a former criminal who later reformed and became a sought-after fraud consultant. (You may have seen his story portrayed by Leonardo DiCaprio in the movie *Catch Me If You Can*.) Frank described the crimes he committed in his younger life as "crimes of opportunity." He explained that he never planned any of his criminal activity (forgery, theft, impersonation of a US Customs official, impersonating a pilot, car theft, etc.). In Frank's words, "The opportunities just presented themselves." Frank of course turned his life around and went on to enjoy a very successful career with the FBI.

WHEN OPEN HOUSE EQUALS OPEN OPPORTUNITY

In early 2021, a well-dressed, well-spoken sixteen-year-old boy was arrested in California accused of stealing $40,000 in jewelry from an open house. The boy had been posing as a millionaire to gain access to multimillion-dollar homes where open houses were being conducted throughout Central and Southern California.

Although an appointment and financial paperwork were required to tour the home, the young boy claimed to be twenty-three and had a letter claiming access to millions of dollars. He was very comfortable speaking to others about high-end homes, investments, and finance.

In the event that led to his arrest, the young man was left alone to walk through the house, and after his departure, it was discovered the homeowner's jewelry had been stolen. The teen had viewed several other homes in the area under the same false pretenses, but he was not left alone at those residences, and no crimes were reported.

After gaining a search warrant for the boy's home, detectives discovered two lists of high-end homes and yachts that the teen visited. Being a minor, he was booked into a juvenile detention center and at the time of this writing was still awaiting trial.

Open house theft is nothing new to our industry. When an opportunist visits an open house, they are usually hoping you will be distracted so *they* can be isolated and have the opportunity to commit the theft. Sometimes they work with accomplices, but usually there is no physical assault involved. By contrast, when a predator comes to an open house, they want to isolate *you,* and it will always end in a physical assault.

Crimes of opportunity are random. Having situational awareness, being perceptive, and paying attention to your environment offers you a chance to react ahead of time if a potential opportunistic threat is coming your way. Victims are usually selected at random, "in the wrong place at the wrong time." Most often a real estate agent's defense in that situation is reactive.

NO SHORTCUTS TO SAFETY

I have studied, deconstructed, and analyzed the crimes committed against real estate professionals in an effort to identify the behavior and patterns of a predator, and to provide you with meaningful insight and a better understanding of the issues we face and solutions that can be put to practical use in informed decision making.

In our industry, there has been a tendency to shortcut this process which has led to poor and ineffective solutions, education, and practices. My analysis has gone beyond just the surface facts. It has revealed identifying signs and behaviors we didn't recognize before.

In order for agents to better protect ourselves from becoming victims, we need a better understanding of the types of crimes committed against us. This allows us to address the questions of *What do we do now?* and *What don't we do?*

> Whether you are male or female, young or old, no one is immune from crime.

Sharing the research findings and assessments is critical when collaborating for safe practices in our industry. You've heard the phrase before, "Knowledge is power." Consider knowledge POTENTIAL power. You have to utilize the knowledge for it to be a powerful tool at your disposal.

Whether you are male or female, young or old, no one is immune from crime. However, there are many ways you can protect yourself from both predatory crimes and crimes of opportunity. I'll be digging deeper into each of these in the coming chapters. Following these practices will take the target off you and keep you from being selected as the next potential victim.

chapter five

A CHILLING DISPLAY

A Texas real estate agent showing a buyer a newly-listed home received the shock of a lifetime when he and his client stepped out on the back deck to look at the backyard. He immediately noticed the unusual shed of a neighboring property—covered with photos of women he recognized as fellow real estate agents.

He quickly notified the local police. When they arrived and investigated further, additional real estate agent photos were discovered lining the backyard fence, alongside photographs of what looked to be animal carcasses.

Police determined that although the site was "very concerning," the owner of the shed hadn't broken any laws, and therefore, no citations were issued. When questioned, the homeowner offered no comment as to why he created the display but stated that "he didn't understand why the shed was causing concern" and agreed to remove the display so the agents involved "could sleep soundly."[1]

The real estate agent who found the shed did the right thing: he reported it. By doing so, he may have saved a life. What is the lesson here?

MASTERY SKILLS

Don't Be a Secret Agent!

If you see something, say something! When you witness something that doesn't look quite right, tell someone. We are all in this profession together, and together we can take control of our safety.

Tell your broker. Tell your local association. Tell your state association. Sharing your story may help someone else. Because of NAR's commitment to the safety of its members, they have created a network for the reporting of incidents that will deploy safety alerts via social media when a physical or cyber threat warrants national attention. You can report a safety incident at *http://nar. realtor/safety/realtor-safety-network.*

THE TESTS YOU WANT TO FAIL

We work hard to become real estate professionals with successful careers. In addition to all of our initial education and testing, we become lifelong students of the industry, testing our knowledge and professionalism along the way in order to keep our licenses active and stay abreast of industry issues, changes, and trends.

There are tests, however, that we all must intentionally fail—the multiple layers of tests that predators run through when selecting their potential targets. To remain successful in the real estate business, agents need to take charge of their own safety and master key safe business practices to make sure you *fail* a predator's tests.

These protection practices may be different from anything you have heard before and were designed to advance the real estate professionals' mastery of safety. They are solutions based and focused on the prevention of real-life predatory crimes facing the real estate industry. Mastering your personal safety is not difficult and will not hinder your success in real estate in any way. Rather, doing so will enhance your business and help ensure you make it home safely at the end of every workday.

PHASE ONE: VICTIM SELECTION

Successful real estate agents often become public figures in the communities they serve. The more successful you become, the more you are in the public eye, and the more your name is remembered when it comes to buying or selling real estate. That is exactly what our marketing is designed to do. However, the marketing that is meant to invite contact from prospective clients is also the same marketing that can unintentionally invite contact from a predator.

Depending on their goal (robbery, rape, murder, etc.), predators look for different things when selecting their victims, but there is often a common denominator—easy, vulnerable targets. When predators search for a specific *type* of victim, they frequently turn to the headshots many agents use to market themselves and gain recognition. There are several documented cases of predators marking up photos of agents in real estate advertisements, often circling headshots of potential targets.

MASTERY SKILLS

Photo Awareness.

Consider marketing yourself without a headshot by creating a clean, sleek, professional look using your company name and logo or your team's name and logo. Keep your photo and photos of others out of it. If you must market with a photo, be aware of what you project in that photo.

Look straight into the camera. A tilt of the head one way or the other shows vulnerability to a predator and can be viewed as submissive. Your smile should say "business authoritative" not be seen as playful or conveying vulnerability, like when looking at a loved one.

These guidelines are not only for females; a male agent is often the target of a predator. **Be aware of what your photos portray.** Designer watches, expensive suits, and fancy cars scream wealth and could be used to target you for robbery. Whether male or female, if you must use a photo, be sure it doesn't showcase valuables or designer products.

Your professional business look should set a tone of business boundaries and may keep the predator from saving your name and photo in a collage of potential targets.

PHASE TWO: CYBERSTALKING

In January 2020, A Texas man was arrested following an investigation of a cyberstalker who was targeting local real estate agents. Additionally, he also targeted and threatened to assault the real estate agent's children, whose names and photos were copied from social media, gaining the attention of the FBI Human Trafficking Division.

Several agents complained of receiving explicit phone calls, text messages, and unusual FaceTime attempts. When he was arrested, the predator was caught in the act of sending lewd, perverse, and threatening messages. The phone calls received were made from phone numbers that the agents didn't recognize. Police state he used apps to mask the number he was calling from.

Investigators working with the Human Trafficking Division further stated that the case was bigger than they had anticipated. The predator had actually been targeting hundreds of real estate agents spanning across twenty-two states.

Following his arrest, the predator's DNA was collected and entered into law enforcements' CODIS database. He was linked to a cold case murder of a twenty-one-year-old female whose body was found partially nude alongside a rural highway. She had been strangled.

Authorities also linked him to yet another murder of a twenty-one-year-old woman whose body was discovered on a rural dirt road one year later. She died of blunt force trauma and was also strangled. She also happened to be the roommate of the first woman found.

The predator died in prison on August 27, 2021, before being formally sentenced.

After a predator has identified and selected his potential targets, he will move on to Phase Two of his victim selection test: cyberstalking. A veil of invisibility and low risk for detection and identification makes cyberstalking far easier, less time-consuming, and more common than physically stalking someone, especially when the predator has many potential targets.

Predators begin by searching for your professional information, company, and contact information before moving on to your private life, home address, and net worth. They will dig deep into your social media accounts and those of your family and friends.

Although cyberstalking may go undetected at this stage, it will eventually lead to actual physical stalking and possible assault.

MASTERY SKILLS

Social Media Savvy.

Keep your professional life professional and your private life private. If you're not sure how publicly exposed and accessible you currently are, do an internet search of yourself. You might be surprised to see results that can provide a roadmap of your life to a predator.

On your social media accounts, **use your full name only on business profiles**. On your personal profiles, use a nickname or an abbreviated version of your name, such as your first and middle name only. Or do what one of my brilliant teacher friends did so his students could not find him online: he spelled his name backwards.

Perform a reverse image search of your business photo to see exactly where it might be found. **Don't use the same photo on your business profile that you use on your personal profile.** Using different photos for business and personal might just throw a predator off the track.

Use your personal email address for your personal accounts and your business email and phone number for professional accounts. Most social media accounts have a feature allowing you to block anyone from searching for you by email or phone.

MASTERY SKILLS

Social Media Friends and Connections.

Make sure your social media *friends* are ones that you wouldn't mind meeting face to face. If that thought provokes an ill feeling with someone on your friends list, delete that person.

Don't accept friend requests from people you don't personally know, including friends of friends. There is no guarantee that your friend knows them very well—or at all! A predator only needs to get on the friends list of one of your unsuspecting friends before showing up as "someone you may know." If you're getting that prompt, so is the predator!

Set your social media accounts to private. That goes for your posts, too! Remember though, just because your account is set to private doesn't mean that your friends' accounts are. **Be aware and careful of posts in which you are tagged.**

Keep your friends list settings, which identifies your relationship to family members, private to keep them from potentially also becoming a target. Facebook is the biggest collector of this information, but it is easy to prevent it through your account settings.

Do not list family members in your profile. You already know who they are. Predators do not need to know who they are. This includes watching what you post in the "life events" section on your Facebook profile, which is automatically set as a public view until you change the settings.

Be careful of check-ins. Do you go to a specific gym or coffee house often? Checking in may alert a predator who then will know when and where to find you. Don't let apps show your location.

Have you been to a really cool place that you want to tell your friends about or post pictures of? **Wait and post it until *after* you have left that location**. This is especially true for anyone vacationing. Why let anyone know that your home is currently vacant?

MASTERY SKILLS

Keep It Professional.

Keep your business–profiles professional. This includes paying attention to what you reveal in your professional bio. You can build a business without divulging information about your spouse or partner, your kids' names or the schools they attend, or even your dog's name.

Disclosing information about your private life will provide a predator with a reason to keep focused on you and studying other members of your family, all of which feed into a predator's high when targeting victims.

Never disclose where you live. Stay away from saying things like, "This is the best subdivision in the city! I know because I also live here."

MASTERY SKILLS

Keep Tabs on Who Else is Posting About You.

Pay attention to what your brokerage posts both on their website and on their social media sites. Brokerages like to put their agents on display, often boasting about agent successes. This well-intentioned practice shows potential clients the wealth of knowledgeable agents available to help with an array of complex real estate transactions.

I know my brokerage and managing broker's social media account is not set to private, so I intentionally elected to opt out. I was asked, "Are you sure? These posts get a lot of attention!" Maybe they do, but attention from whom? Not just potential clients—also potential predators. That wasn't the kind of attention I wanted to attract.

By opting out, I keep my producing stats and the amount of money I make private. Yes, receiving recognition for how hard you work is nice, but not if it falls into the wrong hands. **There are many ways to promote an agent without revealing how much money they produce.**

Opting out of this practice has resulted in no detrimental loss in my business at all. Agents and brokerages should understand that they may be unintentionally bringing the wrong kind of attention to a specific group of agents.

MASTERY SKILLS

Watch Your Language!

The phrasing we choose to use in marketing can influence and encourage personal interactions that may not be safe. Always take into consideration the mindset of a predator.

I quickly scrolled a very well-known real estate website and within ten seconds found the following information next to a photo of a young lady in what appeared to be a very fun photoshoot, judging by her playful pose:

> I concentrate on providing my clients with 24/7 availability. I often work with clients until late in the evening, as long as they need me, because I understand that high-quality service requires time—and sometimes a lot of it. I also understand the importance of having an agent who is open-minded, willing to listen, and will keep you first on the priority list! Thanks for taking the time to get to know me. I hope I get the opportunity to know you too!

The true prospective client mindset might look at that profile message and think, "Wow, she is available 24/7! She understands that I need attention and I should come first. She's open-minded and will listen to what I have to say. She sounds like a nice person."

But if you re-read that agent's words with the mindset of a predator, what meanings might they convey?

The above information would be better reworded to get the intended meaning across without the ambiguity of the messaging:

> As a real estate professional, I understand timing is important. I work a flexible schedule by appointment. My extensive market knowledge and uncompromising integrity help to ensure your success in the real estate market.

Is the language you are using in your personal marketing and profiles making you a target? **Review your marketing messages** and make any necessary changes that leave no doubt in what your message conveys.

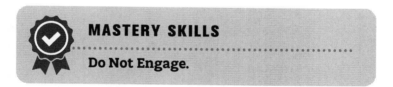

MASTERY SKILLS

Do Not Engage.

Never engage with someone who starts to harass you online or by text. A predator may test your patience and try to engage you before moving on to the next step by sending messages that may cause fear for your personal safety or the safety of others. This feeds into a predator's need for power and control.

If you find yourself a victim of cyberstalking, report it to the police and keep a journal of every piece of harassment received. Having a detailed account will provide a timeline for the police to follow. Stalking is not just one incident. It is a pattern and may lead to the next step of physical stalking.

PHYSICAL STALKING

At some point, a predator is going to feel confident in their choice or choices of potential victims and will take stalking out of cyberspace and into the real world. Sometimes this starts with harassing phone calls or letters. It may be that the predator poses as a potential client, either buyer or seller. This is the last test a predator will run before actually planning the attack, so your failure of this test is absolutely critical.

A Wisconsin real estate agent was stalked for nearly a year by a pair of brothers. These predators sent letters to several homeowners who had listed their property for sale with this particular agent. The letters conveyed a threat that the sellers' homes would be burned down and they would be killed if they didn't terminate their contract with this agent and find someone else to sell their homes.

The brothers also stalked the real estate agent's sister, who happened to be an agent as well. The sisters, who frequently hosted open houses together, started noticing two men appearing regularly at different open houses.

Though they always used fictitious names, the brothers made the mistake at one event of using their real home address on the guest registry. They were finally caught. The predators were charged with two counts of felony stalking and three counts of felony threat to injure.

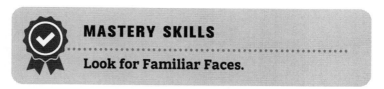

MASTERY SKILLS

Look for Familiar Faces.

Pay attention if the same prospective buyer is frequenting your open houses, especially if the homes are not similar in amenities and price. You may find yourself suddenly bumping into a predator in more than one place.

The predator may show up at an open house you are hosting to identify if you work alone, or could be parked nearby your office checking to see if you are at the office alone, noting your arrival and departure times. He or she may just drive past your office to see if your car is there. Remember, the predator is looking for an easy target.

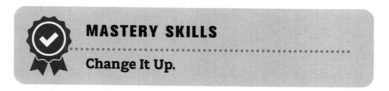

MASTERY SKILLS

Change It Up.

If you have a habit of going to the same coffee shop or grocery store on a regular basis at a predictable time, scan for familiar faces that seem to show up again and again. It could be a predator familiarizing himself with your routine.

Don't become a creature of habit and pattern. Vary your routine. Arrive at the office at different times of the day. Limit your after-hours time working alone in the office. There are numerous accounts of a predator crossing names off of their target list simply because the agent was always around other people, thus becoming a difficult target for the predator.

PHASE THREE: PLANNING THE ATTACK

As mentioned in Chapter Four, this phase of planning the attack is the fantasy stage and may run simultaneously with stalking. The predator has identified a list of potential victims who have passed all of the previous tests and could already be tracking them.

At this stage, the predator is planning and identifying methods of how to get you isolated. A "chance meeting" with you intoxicates the predator at this stage. They enjoy these brief encounters before revealing their true selves.

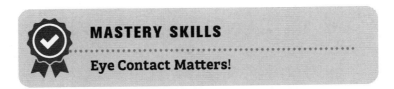

MASTERY SKILLS

Eye Contact Matters!

When someone is near you that you are not familiar with, **make eye contact with the person and don't smile.** Maintain a neutral facial expression. Put them on notice that they are no longer invisible and have been recognized.

Now, this part may sound silly to you, but it is important. When breaking eye contact with a potential predator, do not look down. This is considered submissive in the predator's eye. On the flip side of that, don't look up. This can be construed as you thinking you are above them or better than them. It could be enough to trigger them and incite an attack. Instead, break eye contact by looking to the side. This is considered neutral. I will share more about reading non-verbal language in the pages to come.

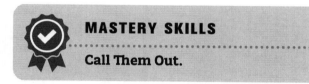

MASTERY SKILLS
Call Them Out.

If you notice that you are seeing the same person repeatedly, and you are in the company of others, **call them out**. "I've noticed you at a couple of open houses," or, "Hey, I saw you at the coffee house today." This not only lets them know you are on to them, but others now are aware as well, which throws them off their plan of surprise.

Don't pay attention to the lies that follow when the predator responds to you. **Stay in charge!** Don't change your stance or your facial expression. You have just become a challenge to the predator and are no longer an easy target.

PHASE FOUR: EXECUTING THE ATTACK

A California male real estate agent was shot and killed during a home invasion, and three suspects were arrested. On a Sunday morning, a neighbor of the agent noticed a vehicle going up and down their block. The neighbor witnessed a driver dropping off two men before circling the vehicle back around.

The two men approached the side door of the home where the agent lived. When the agent answered the door, the two men confronted him and pushed the agent back into his home, closing the door behind them.

The neighbor immediately notified the police. By the time police arrived, the two men were gone, and the agent was found gagged, bound, and deceased. Details about exactly how the agent died were not released, but the police did release a statement saying, "This was not a random crime. Further information gathered during the investigation points to the agent being specifically targeted."[2] The two men and the driver were eventually caught and charged with homicide.

MASTERY SKILLS

Don't Be a Distracted Driver.

Pay attention to your drive home and keep from making important, engaging phone calls that can keep you distracted. **Vary your route home**. A predator is looking for consistency. If you feel like you are being followed, drive directly to a police station.

At some point, stalking and fantasy no longer provide

an intoxicating high for the predator. It is at this time the predator decides who the victim will be, picks a location, and plans the meeting. The predator spends very little time in this phase. He or she feels ready and completely detached from any humanity of those they are about to assault.

In most cases, this phase begins with a phone call to arrange a meeting for a showing. It is here you will have your first opportunity to assess the prospect or predator, the risks, the property, and the overall situation.

As technology and consumer solutions continue to evolve in the real estate industry, real estate information is now readily available on the internet for consumers to access and view publicly. Therefore, it makes sense that for many buyers, the home buying process begins with an internet search. Professional photographs showcase homes, giving prospective buyers an intimate look into a home from the comfort of their couch.

Unfortunately, this gives predators the same intimate look as they filter through their search for a vacant home. It used to be that real estate agents were warned to never reveal a home is vacant in marketing. With so many photos now online, that becomes more difficult to avoid, making it easier for predators to pick their vacant location.

MASTERY SKILLS

Keep the Lived-In Look.

Consider photographing a home that will be going on the market before furniture and belongings are removed. If that is not possible, consider making use of virtual staging when listing vacant homes for sale. A quick internet search will reveal software and other sources to accomplish this. In addition to potentially making a predator move on, you'll have a very happy seller who appreciates all your professionalism in providing extra services that help make their home sell faster.

MASTERY SKILLS

Communicate the Vacancy with Other Agents.

It is equally important to **disclose to agents who will be showing the property that it is vacant.** You can disclose this information so it is not available to the public, either through a Broker Remarks field in the listing itself or right in the showing instructions to the agent showing the property.

MASTERY SKILLS

Ditch the Sign.

Putting a sign in front of a vacant home for sale can bring unwanted attention, especially if it is noticed that no one is coming or going from the property. **If a**

home is vacant, consider removing the sign from the front yard.

I have personally had two vacant homes for sale recently, in two very different areas, become the target of thieves. After the signs were removed, however, there was never another robbery attempt even while the homes were still being marketed on the internet. They both sold in record time. (Fortunately, they both also had security systems.)

It may happen that, despite all of your efforts to fail a predator's tests, you still have an unexpected encounter. If that happens, you still have some lines of defense. Predators need to have control over the victims they choose and don't expect a victim to be prepared. In the coming chapters, I will share what you need to know to take control and be prepared for a variety of possible interactions with a potential predator.

CHAPTER FIVE MASTERY SKILLS SUMMARY

1. Don't Be a Secret Agent!

- ► If you see something, say something!

2. Photo Awareness

- ► Consider marketing yourself without a headshot.
- ► Look straight into the camera.
- ► Be aware of what your photos portray.

3. Social Media Savvy

- ► Keep your professional life professional and your private life private.
- ► Use your full name only on business profiles.
- ► Perform a reverse image search of your business photo.
- ► Don't use the same photo on your business profile that you use on your personal profile.
- ► Use your personal email address for your personal accounts and your business email and phone number for professional accounts.

4. Social Media Friends and Connections

- ► Make sure your social media "friends" are ones that you wouldn't mind meeting face to face.
- ► Don't accept friend requests from people you don't personally know.
- ► Set your social media accounts to private.

- ► Be aware and careful of posts in which you are tagged.
- ► Keep your friends list settings, which identifies your relationship to family members, private.
- ► Do not list family members in your profile.
- ► Be careful of check-ins. Wait and post it until *after* you have left that location.

5. Keep It Professional

- ► Keep your business-profiles professional.
- ► Never disclose where you live.

6. Keep Tabs on Who Else is Posting About You

- ► Pay attention to what your brokerage posts both on their website and on their social media sites.
- ► There are many ways to promote an agent without revealing how much money they produce.

7. Watch Your Language!

- ► The phrasing we choose to use in marketing can influence and encourage personal interactions that may not be safe.
- ► Review your marketing messages.

8. Do Not Engage

- ► Never engage with someone who starts to harass you online or by text.

9. Look for Familiar Faces

► Pay attention if the same prospective buyer is frequenting your open houses.

10. Change It Up

► Don't become a creature of habit and pattern.
► Vary your routine.

11. Eye Contact Matters!

► Make eye contact with the person and don't smile.

12. Call Them Out

► Call them out.
► Stay in Charge.

13. Don't Be a Distracted Driver

► Pay attention to your drive home.
► Vary your route home.

14. Keep the Lived-In Look

► Consider photographing a home that will be going on the market before furniture and belongings are removed.

15. Communicate the Vacancy with Other Agents

► Disclose to agents who will be showing the property that it is vacant.

16. Ditch the Sign

► If a home is vacant, consider removing the sign from the front yard.

chapter six

QUESTIONS THAT CAN SAVE YOUR LIFE

A potential buyer called a female real estate agent in California and explained that he and his wife were interested in a particular home. The agent arranged to meet the man and his wife at the home the following morning.

Upon arrival, the agent noticed the wife was not present for the showing. The husband apologized, stating his wife was unable to join them because she had been called in to work. The real estate agent, feeling uneasy, opened the front door and told the buyer to go ahead and take a look at the home as she waited outside. The real estate agent waited approximately ten to fifteen minutes before she opened the front door and entered the home, just as the buyer was coming down the stairs from the second floor.

While she was still standing by the front door, the man managed to shut the door behind her and pulled out a gun. He pointed the gun to her head and told her to get on the ground. He then bound her wrists and ankles, put his knees on her chest, and asked her where her purse was. After the agent told him that her purse was in the car, he grabbed her car keys and cell phone and went outside to locate her purse.

While the predator was outside retrieving her purse, the agent was able to break free of her bindings. This angered the predator; he again bound her wrists and ankles, and this time demanded the PIN to her ATM card. The agent complied with his requests and told him to just go ahead and take everything she had in hopes he would just rob her and leave her alone. She told the predator she had a little boy at home that needed her, and that being a single mom, she is all he had.

The predator directed the agent up the stairs in the home to a walk-in closet. There he made her remove her clothing. He then raped and beat her repeatedly with his fists and the butt of his gun. Afterward, he told her, "I am going to kill you now."[1] The agent wondered why he didn't shoot her. It was at this time she decided to fight back!

During the struggle, the agent noticed the gun started to fall apart to the point that it was no longer in his hand. Tired from the struggle, the predator pulled out a knife and started to stab the agent with it, at one point holding it up to her throat. The agent blocked his efforts with her hand. He sliced right through it, to the bone. During the struggle, the agent was able to get away and run to a bathroom where she tried to close the door in an attempt to lock herself in. Overpowering her, the predator was able to keep her from closing the bathroom door by shoving it open so hard that it knocked her inside the bathtub.

Although the agent was hurt badly with lacerations all over her body, she remained conscious, but she no longer could find the strength to fight. The predator pulled her from the bathroom back to the closet floor where she begged him to leave and to just let her die. The predator left the room, and although she could no longer see him, she could hear him still in the house, picking up items and possibly cleaning up the crime scene. He then returned to the closet, where the agent pretended to be dead, and stabbed her again in the neck and stomach.

When the agent could no longer hear the predator in the home and felt sure that he was gone from the property, she managed to get outside, screaming for help as she collapsed. She soon would hear a voice saying that an ambulance was on the way.

The agent's injuries were so severe that she needed a blood transfusion. She had to undergo many surgeries over a period of two years, suffered from major nerve damage, had to have three discs removed in her spine, and had a titanium plate placed in her neck. She could no longer bend her fingers in her hand and no longer had any feeling in them.

But she survived.

A blood pattern from the scene of the attack quickly led police to a nearby home where the predator was living. Evidence was found in and around the home, including the gun he used for the attack, his blood-stained clothing, and the agent's belongings. The police determined that the gun the predator used was actually a BB gun. When the police interrogated the predator, he gave them a narrative of the events that matched those the agent had told police.[2]

The predator was sentenced to ninety-one years to life in prison. According to prosecutors, the predator found the agent by doing an internet search. He spotted her photo and contacted her about viewing the foreclosed home.[3]

Predators will often assess a potential target during the initial contact to set the meeting, and exhibit similar cues to their intentions.

PEOPLE SAY EXACTLY WHAT THEY MEAN

Hopefully, by now you have done your homework from the previous chapters. You have a better understanding of the types of crimes committed against real estate agents, the predator's cycle when choosing their victim(s), and how to fail their tests. And you have put your mastery skills to work for you to stay off a predator's radar.

Now, when you get a phone call or a lead from a buyer or seller that you don't know, what do you do?

MASTERY SKILLS

Ask Questions...Then Listen
Carefully to the Answers.

Not everyone is a predator; most people are honest, legitimate, buyers and sellers. We ask potential clients questions to better understand their needs so we can best serve them. A potential buyer or seller will honestly answer—without much thought or hesitation—and we are able to move forward.

However, **when we ask a predator questions, he or she has many decisions to make before answering.** Which information will they share? Which information will they withhold? They not only have to be careful of their word choices but must also be aware that any statements they make may throw them off balance and tip us off. They have to do all of this in less than a milli-second while we wait for a reply.

That is why it is important that after you ask a question, you patiently wait for the reply no matter how much time passes. Do not try to fill the silence while waiting for the reply. A predator may have an idea of what kind of questions we might ask, but they won't be ready to talk through the *type* of questions we might ask, which we will discuss later in this chapter.

We know we can't always tell the difference between a predator or potential client by what they look like, but there are ways to tell by what they sound like. This process is called Statement Analysis® (created by U.S. Marshall Mark McClish). Statement Analysis® is the process of analyzing a person's words to see if he or she is being truthful or deceptive. While it can take years to learn these scientific, investigative tech-niques, you don't need to be an expert to expose a poten-tial predator.

We'll concentrate on the root of Statement Analysis® with a couple of simple skills. **Simply paying atten-tion to what is said and noting changes in the speed of speech, volume, and pitch will help you recognize**

verbal red flags that occur in most deceptive statements. The process we will use will not only serve us well when contacted by a potential client, but will also help to serve that client later by having accurate client records.

> Protecting and promoting the best interest of your client depends greatly on your having the right information.

A predator, though, may have a little tougher time getting past this process, as most falsehoods quickly unravel simply by asking the right questions.

Never ignore dishonesty from a prospect. Probe deeper and ask questions. After all, protecting and promoting the best interest of your client depends greatly on your having the right information.[4] If you don't have the truth to work with, you're not able to service or represent your client well.

MASTERY SKILLS

It's Not Just What They Say, but *How* They Say It.

Listen carefully. Everything a person says has meaning. What they don't say has meaning as well. Listening is a challenging skill for most of us. Our brains will often fill in a conversation, interpreting words we want to hear before the speaker is even finished talking. Some of us may even jump in while the speaker is still speaking, blurting out what they think is going to be said, and then the speaker responds, "That's not what I was going to say at all!" We tend to guess and fill in the blanks on our own instead of allowing others to speak. That practice can be especially dangerous for the real estate agent trying to avoid a predator.

The voice is a built-in lie detector. Have you ever played two truths and a lie? One player tells three short stories or shares three statements about themself. Two are true; one is a lie. The other players ask questions to try and decipher which story or statement is a lie. Many times, players will listen to the statement or story being told and judge its deception by how outrageous the story is that is being told. **Truth seekers understand that there are also verbal deception indicators lurking in the tone and speech of a deceptive person**. They don't have to know the whole story; they can tell by just listening to the voice of the storyteller.

When there is a sudden change in a person's pattern of speech, that may indicate there may be something to pay attention to. Suppose you have a fast talker who suddenly slows down as if they are trying to think of what to say. There is a possibility that they are trying to keep from telling you something—like the truth—and trying to remember the lie they need to go in its place. On the other hand, if you have a slow talker who suddenly talks much faster, there could be something they are trying to skip over or cover up.

Likewise, the tone of a person's voice has meaning, as well. **Vocal tone is related to emotions and is one of the most powerful indicators of deception.** Vocal tone rises when a person is excited or angry. On the flip side, the vocal tone will lower if a person is sad, depressed, or shamed. When your potential client's tone changes, pay attention! We tend to notice and react when someone's voice gets higher, but if your potential client's voice goes lower, that could be a dangerous red flag!

Another deceptive tactic is leaving part of the story out—where there seems to be a beginning and an end but not much in the middle. Why is information omitted? Get into the habit of asking yourself, *What are they not saying here? What are they keeping from me and why?*

> Get into the habit of asking yourself, *What are they not saying here? What are they keeping from me and why?*

Practice your truth-detecting skills at home with friends or family or have a little fun with your colleagues at the office by playing two truths and a lie. See how often you can spot the lie. The more you practice, the more often you will be able to recognize the truth from the lie. It's worth noting that if someone is thinking of a real story or event that happened some time ago, they may have to pause or slow down while trying to recall the memory. But with practice, you will be able to spot the difference between *remembering* and *fabricating* in no time.

MASTERY SKILLS

The Predator's Balancing Act.

Inconsistencies in a conversation can often be picked up by shifts in tense and word choice. Think of a deceptive person as a person on a balance beam. Their challenge is to remain upright and make steady progress to get across that beam without any slip-ups, to the other side of your skepticism.

A deceptive person carries with them heavy baggage of deceit:

1. The truth

2. The lie

3. The blended partial fact of their lie

4. What they may have told you in previous conversations

5. Any new facts or lies that they now want you to believe

6. A fear of what you may have discovered already but have not disclosed yet

This extra baggage of deceit will likely throw them off balance if you're paying attention. **Your job is to watch for imbalances (or leaks of the deception).** While on a balance beam, a gymnast might throw out one leg to compensate for the weight and balance of the other. That's what a deceitful person will do with their speech. It will start to waver and shift in uncharacteristic ways. You'll be able to hear uncertainty when people aren't telling the truth. An inexperienced person on a balance beam may not try to reclaim their balance at all but try to make it all the way across your skepticism with speed instead. An aggressive communicator leaves you little time to think. **Regain control of the conversation and slow it down by repeating your question. Break up the conversation by interrupting if needed.**

When you hear things like, "My hand to God" or "I swear on so and so's grave", those are convincing tactics. Ask yourself, *Why do I need to be convinced here?*

Truthful people will convey information. Deceptive people need to convince you the information is true. When you hear things like, "My hand to God" or "I swear on so and so's grave", those are convincing tactics. Ask yourself, *Why do I need to be convinced here?*

When a gymnast suddenly stops on the balance beam, they attempt to reclaim their balance and start down the beam again with grace. Similarly, **a dramatic pause mid-conversation is an indication that a person may be trying to recall the deception that must be put in place of the truth.** A deceptive person will stop mid-sentence (realize they are about to say something they don't want you to know) will not move forward and instead, immediately take that conversation in a different direction.

We've only covered the very basics here, but once you practice listening, you'll be surprised at how much you actually pick up from one single conversation. We can make this even easier with buyer/seller safety systems.

SIMPLE BUYER/SELLER SAFETY SYSTEMS

Rather than simply gathering information from a prospective client on the phone to secure your next appointment, start a conversation with the potential client. No one likes to be interrogated with a list of questions, but we can ask intentional questions through normal conversation.

MASTERY SKILLS

Carefully Interview Potential Buyers.

Use a client intake form to record the information provided by the prospective client each and every time, for every client, *no exceptions*! Not only will your client appreciate your attention to detail, but this will also help you accommodate a growing client base and come in handy in remembering the intel gathered when meeting with the client face-to-face at a later date.

Ask open-ended questions that can't be answered simply by saying yes or no. When asked open-ended questions that require an extended response, a predator's words will betray them. Responses that require an extended reply, will help you find out the *why, how,* and *what* they are thinking.

By asking closed-ended questions, such as those that require a simple yes or no, you won't get any information to analyze. Save these questions for the end of the intake questionnaire. **When asking open-ended questions, listen for any inconsistencies.** You may be spotting a lie, but you are really searching for the truth. Our brains automatically want to tell the truth, so someone who must stick to a lie will stumble. The more the potential client speaks, the more information you will have to analyze, and the easier it will be to tell if they are being truthful or not.

Here are some sample open-ended buyer questions to ask:

1. *I appreciate your reaching out to me today, can you tell me how you found me?* If the answer is that they found you on the internet, ask another open-ended question....

2. *Oh? On what site did you find me?* If they say they cannot remember, you can ask the next question....

3. *What was it about me that made you decide to contact me?* When a client does decide that you are the best to represent them, there is a compelling reason why they picked you, and they will be able to tell you what it was. If they can't tell you, you must dig deeper. You can also ask....

4. *Where do you live now? Are you renting or do you own the residence?*

5. *Why are you moving?* If the prospect states they just want to see a particular home, ask questions like...

6. *What is it about that home that interests you?*

7. *How long have you been looking?*

8. *Are you pre-qualified/pre-approved?* If yes, ask them to email a copy of their pre-approval certificate directly to you. If not, explain to them that even if they found a home today that they loved, a seller nowadays will not accept a contract without a pre-approval certificate. You can take this even further and let them know how important being pre-approved is for ensuring you are searching in the right price range. Offer to help them in that process *before* meeting them.

Setting them up for success and positioning them in the best light is part of being a real estate professional. Don't be afraid of losing someone who is just curious and not serious. Realize that a buyer will naturally want to make sure they can get approved for a mortgage first and know for how much. Being pre-approved to purchase is a natural first step when purchasing a new home. If the intention is not to purchase, this step is skipped and should be considered a red flag.

9. If the potential buyer states, *I'm only in town for the day,* ask if they set up any other showing appointments, and if so, where and with whom? Ask yourself what kind of buyer comes into town for the day and doesn't set an appointment first to see if the showing is even possible or if the home is even available to show? Explore their buying motive.

10. If the potential buyer states they will be paying cash, understand that requiring proof of funds to purchase is the same as being prequalified. Ask them to send you proof of funds *before* meeting with them. You will also need this information when presenting an offer.

Getting these necessary questions answered provides you with an opportunity to be of service to a client. It also gives you an idea of how motivated they are, where they are in the process, and what you will need to prepare for them.

Be sure to adjust your questions so they flow with the conversation. Again, no one likes to feel like they are being interrogated. You can always skip a question on the intake form and go back to it to keep the fluidity of the conversation going.

Some potential buyers carry a sense of urgency to run out and see a home immediately, especially if market conditions help create an urgency where newly-listed homes are going fast. **Don't shortcut your safety!** Relieve the buyers' fears by letting them know that you are going to speak with the listing agent to set the showing appointment and call them back.

A predator won't wait. |

This not only gives you time to set the showing appointment, but it also gives you some time to check out your prospect. Call the listing agent and ask how long offers will be considered and if there is a cutoff date/time you need to know. Ask them how many offers they currently have on the home. This information will dictate how much time you have to work with. The key here is to buy yourself a little time for a safety check-up. A predator won't wait. It throws their plan off and they are no longer in control. A prospective buyer will understand and await your call. Take a little time, review the information on your intake form, make sure that everything adds up and check out your prospect.

What if you are the listing agent? Well, you'll already know the answers to the questions above and have some control by being able to directly communicate with the seller to set a showing appointment, while still giving yourself enough time to check out the prospective buyer.

MASTERY SKILLS

Sellers Can Be Predators, Too... So Interview Them Carefully!

Some predators will go as far as posing as a home seller. A real estate agent in Newark was contacted by a potential seller, requesting an appointment to list his property. During the call, the potential seller mentioned that he had seen her picture, thought she was pretty, and he remembered her. This made the agent feel uncomfortable about meeting with him alone, so she took a fellow agent with her to the listing appointment.

When they arrived at the property, there was a van parked and running in front of the house. When speaking with the person in the van, he mentioned that the owner was running late and that he was there to help the owner move some things. When the owner arrived, he was very insistent that the agents see the bedrooms in the home and showed them to the loft. Once they were all in the loft, one of the agents tried to turn on the light but noticed it was taped off. So she turned on a light she had on her cell phone. They immediately noticed that there was someone in the bed and began to run.

As they were trying to open the door to get out of the home, the door handle had been loosened and came off, but the agents were able to run out through the garage. Once they were out safely, they did call the police and found out the seller had a 20-year history of criminal activity from assault to sexual imposition. The agents share their story with other real estate professionals to bring awareness that this kind of incident can happen, and if something doesn't feel right, proceed with caution.

Here are some sample open-ended questions to ask when vetting a prospective seller:

1. *I appreciate your reaching out to me today, can you tell me how you found me?* If the answer is that they found you on the internet, ask another open-ended question...

2. *Oh? What site did you find me on?*

3. *What was it about me that made you decide to contact me?* Again, when a client does decide that you are the best to represent them, there is a compelling reason why they picked you. They will be able to tell you what it was. If they can't tell you, you must dig deeper.

4. *Why are you moving?* The answer will also let you know if this is a distressed sale where emotions may be high.

5. *Tell me about your current home.*

6. *How long have you owned it?*

7. *Have there been any improvements to the home since you purchased it?*

8. *Who is listed on the title/deed?*

9. *Will all decision-makers be available at your listing appointment?*

Listen to how questions are being received and replied to. A client that is calling on the expertise of a real estate professional has no problem explaining exactly what it is that they need and appreciate being guided in the process.

A predator's goal, however, is to catch you off guard. One way to do that is to gain your trust. They may try calling you and saying, "Hi! Remember me? You showed me a home last year! You were so professional, and I am finally in a position to purchase. I'd like to work with you." If you do not remember this person at all, ask questions!

1. *Which home did I show you?* If they say they cannot remember the street name, this could be a red flag. Press on!

2. *How did we meet again?* If it still is unfamiliar, that is red flag #2

3. *Did I show you (make up an address)?* If they say yes, that is a red flag on fire!

One last word of caution before moving forward. **Predators are known to practice, too!** They will phone different real estate agents, learn the ropes, and practice skills until they get it right. If your vetting process asks open-ended questions, making you a hard target, the predator will move on to an easier target.

If you feel comfortable after the seller interview, set an appointment, but give yourself at least a day in between speaking to them and meeting with them at their home. After all, you will need some time to gather enough data to provide a comparative market analysis. Before meeting at the home, make sure to check the tax records to identify the rightful owner of the home. Make sure to also check the sales history of the home.

1. **Use the county websites to search tax records** to see who pays the tax bills on the home. If their name is not on the tax bill, you should ask them why.

2. **Check county records for ownership of the home**. Make sure the person you are dealing with owns the home. If more than one person is on the deed or title, make sure all decision-makers will be present at the appointment.

3. **Be extra careful in estate situations.** Although there is an executor of the estate, often there is more than one person that has an interest in the home. Ask for the names and contact information of all interested parties and check them out too. Another word of caution here; estate sales are often emotional. Make a point of asking the executor if anyone is against the sale. Offer to make yourself available to have a conversation with that person to alleviate any fears they may have and gain a perspective or a better understanding of the process.

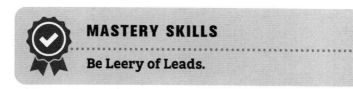

MASTERY SKILLS

Be Leery of Leads.

Take extra precautions when working with buyer/seller leads and understand that they are exactly what they say they are—a *lead* of someone who may be considering buying or selling. Unless you have an agreement in place prior to receiving these leads, understand that more than likely the potential prospect has not been properly vetted. **Use the same buyer/seller intake safety system for direct calls.**

An agent in Wisconsin regularly purchases leads through some well-known real estate platforms. When she has too many, she will pass a few on to trusted co-workers. She passed a lead to one of her male co-workers who showed the prospective buyer a home. After the showing, the co-worker had a difficult time reaching the prospective buyer again. Later that week, that prospective buyer made the news. He had been arrested on kidnapping and sexual assault charges.

The agent who originally received the lead stated she couldn't imagine what might have happened to her had she shown this predator the home situated on a couple of acres out in the country with no neighbors. She sent a message describing what had happened to fellow agents, encouraging them to remain vigilant.

MASTERY SKILLS

Do Your Due Diligence!

You now have the time to **investigate all the information the prospect gave you over the phone and make sure they are legitimate.**

1. Review the conversation with the information you took down on your intake form while it is fresh in your mind. Does the information all line up? Did any red flags jump out at you?

2. Do a reverse phone number search and make sure the number they called from actually does belong to them. (Most internet results will also give you a prospect's address.)

3. Enter their name in a search engine; often this will also lead you to their social media pages. Check out their social media profiles.

4. A predator will often claim they are a professor, a doctor, or a lawyer. If you cannot find them on the web, that is a red flag.

5. Anyone with a computer can fake a pre-approval certificate. Call the lender on the pre-approval certificate. Don't just call the name and number on the certificate. Search for the mortgage office online, then call that number and ask to speak to the name of the loan officer that was provided. But don't stop there...

6. Tell the loan officer you have a client in common. Ask the lender how far in the process this buyer is. Did the lender just gather information from the prospect over the phone and base the pre-approval off that, or did they verify assets and employment, etc.? Although a lender will hold personal information personal, these are questions easy to answer without violating any privacy regulations.

I once spoke with a lender I have never heard of before when given a pre-approval from a prospective buyer client. I searched for the mortgage company online then called the toll-free number posted and asked for the loan officer by name. I asked the same questions I advised you to ask. I wasn't asking for any personal information. When I heard hesitation in his voice, I explained that not only did I need to position the client's offer in the best possible light, but I also schooled him on agent safety.

He replied by stating he had no idea these types of crimes were being committed against real estate agents. He then assured me that he had worked with this person for a couple of months and had income tax records, verified employment with his employer, copies of their bank statements and driver's license, etc.

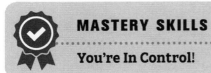

MASTERY SKILLS

You're In Control!

You've done your due diligence. Does everything check out? Great! **Set the appointment. You're in control! Pick the best time given your and the prospect's schedules.** Predators like to gain control immediately. If they can't control the plan, they are flustered and frustrated.

Let them tell you their availability, but you pick the time! For example, they may say "I get off work at 5:00, and it's on my way home, so I'll be there at 5:15."

You might say, "I'll meet you at 5:30." Even though you may be able to accommodate their choice of time, you are letting them know right from the beginning that you are taking control. And if you take control, they lose control. It throws their planning off.

A true buyer understands that everyone has a schedule to work with, and you have more than one client to attend to. You can further deter a potential predator by stating, "We will have 15 minutes at that property to walk through the home before the sellers arrive home or before the next showing." Having such a brief period alone in the property doesn't allow the time needed for a predator to isolate you or attack you and leave undetected.

If things do not add up, if the prospect is not pre-approved, if you don't feel comfortable, if this prospect is not a match for you—don't be afraid to walk away! It is okay to not agree to meet with them. You may have just avoided a bad situation. Safety precautions put you in control of your business, the interaction with the public, and most of all, your safety! Safety systems give you the time to do your due diligence, listen to your instincts, and may just expose a predator.

There is no one way of telling who has ill intentions toward you. But there are a multitude of pre-attack indicators that predators unknowingly display. It is imperative that we train ourselves to recognize these signals in order to prevent a crime from being committed against us and to narrow the processing time between observation and action.

CHAPTER SIX MASTERY SKILLS SUMMARY

1. Ask Questions...Then Listen Carefully to the Answers

► When we ask a predator questions, he or she has many decisions to make before answering. That is why it is important that after you ask a question, you patiently wait for the reply no matter how much time passes.

► Simply paying attention to what is said and noting changes in the speed of speech, volume, and pitch will help you recognize verbal red flags that occur in most deceptive statements.

► Do not try to fill the silence while waiting for the reply.

► Never ignore dishonesty from a prospect.

2. It's Not Just What They Say, but *How* They Say It.

► The voice is a built-in lie detector.

► Truth seekers understand that there are also verbal deception indicators lurking in the tone and speech of a deceptive person.

► When there is a sudden change in a person's pattern of speech, that may indicate there may be something to pay attention to.

► Vocal tone is related to emotions and is one of the most powerful indicators of deception.

3. The Predator's Balancing Act

- ► Inconsistencies in a conversation can often be picked up by shifts in tense and word choice.
- ► Your job is to watch for imbalances (or leaks of the deception).
- ► Regain control of the conversation and slow it down by repeating your question.
- ► Break up the conversation by interrupting if needed.
- ► Truthful people will convey information.
- ► Deceptive people need to convince you the information is true.
- ► A dramatic pause mid-conversation is an indication that a person may be trying to recall the deception that must be put in place of the truth.

4. Carefully Interview Potential Buyers

- ► Use a client intake form to record the information provided by the prospective client each and every time, for every client, no exceptions!
- ► Ask open-ended questions that can't be answered simply by saying yes or no.
- ► When asking open-ended questions, listen for any inconsistencies.
- ► Be sure to adjust your questions so they flow with the conversation.
- ► Don't shortcut your safety!

5. Sellers Can Be Predators, Too... So Interview Them Carefully!

- ► A predator's goal is to catch you off guard.
- ► Predators are known to practice, too!
- ► Use the county websites to search tax records.
- ► Check county records for ownership of the home.
- ► Be extra careful in estate situations.

6. Be Leery of Leads

- ► Take extra precautions when working with buyer/seller leads.
- ► Use the same buyer/seller intake safety system for direct calls.

7. Do Your Due Diligence!

- ► Investigate all the information the prospect gave you over the phone and make sure they are legitimate.

8. You're In Control!

- ► Set the appointment. You're in control!
- ► Pick the best time given your and the prospect's schedules.
- ► Don't be afraid to walk away.

BODY LANGUAGE AND OTHER NON-VERBAL TELLS

When a female real estate agent was attacked outside a home in Los Angeles, it was caught on camera. She recognized the man from an open house the week prior to her attack. He made her feel so uneasy at that open house that she asked a friend to accompany her the following weekend. The friend obliged, but toward the end of the open house, left a little early.

It wasn't long after the friend left that the predator was standing in front of the agent again. The agent immediately recognized him. Was this a coincidence? Or was this a predator waiting for her to be alone? While he toured the home, she stepped outside where surveillance cameras were recording.

The video footage showed the interactions between them. The predator made several requests, trying to lure the agent back into the house. He first asked if he could show her the closet of the home inside one of the bedrooms.

When the agent declined, he then asked her for water. When she told him he could go back in himself and grab a bottle of water out of the refrigerator, he then requested to use the washroom. The agent declined and made up an excuse that the sellers didn't want anyone using the restroom.

During this interaction, the predator obviously noticed the surveillance camera and looked at it twice before he attacked the agent. We witnessed his body language and got a firsthand look at some of the pre-attack indicators we will review throughout this chapter, as well as the agent's involuntary response. The video can be viewed on YouTube at the following link: bit.ly/NTP_attack.[1]

Police did apprehend the predator and charged him with felony assault with a deadly weapon (bodily force) along with four separate misdemeanors. After the video went viral, two other real estate agents came forward with accusations of being groped by the same man at other open houses. The predator was eventually found mentally incompetent and set free.

Whether you are at the office, with clients, or out with friends, the body language of others around you speaks volumes. From eye behavior to where feet are directed, body language can reveal what a person is really thinking. There is no one way of telling just by a glance if someone is a predator or not. Instead, we concentrate on how a person makes us feel *along with* trusting our gut feeling and looking for a cluster of warning signs that reveal a person may not have our best interest at heart.

Before we dissect the video footage of the attack on one of our own, we'll need to gain insight into the hidden secrets our bodies reveal.

NON-VERBAL INTELLIGENCE

In real estate, the path to clear communication with our customers and clients is incalculable. The skill of negotiation is monumental to our success and fundamental to performing fiduciary duties in protecting and serving buyers and sellers.

We negotiate with clients, with vendors, with our brokerages, on listing appointments, and even with ourselves. We negotiate *all the time*! One of the most important negotiations we can enter is the one we struggle with internally; it determines the quality of our life and has a significant impact on our industry.

It is the negotiation of our personal safety.

Words may be considered our primary method of communication, but it is not the only method. When we interact and communicate with each other, we communicate on two levels, verbal and non-verbal. Master negotiators know how to choose their words carefully while negotiating. They understand that body language speaks the loudest and yet is often overlooked.

Non-verbal communication should reinforce what is being said. Because it is done unconsciously, the way individuals communicate nonverbally, or through their body language, may provide the first indication of an underlying issue. Generally, words convey only 7% of what you say; the remaining 93 % is non-verbal.

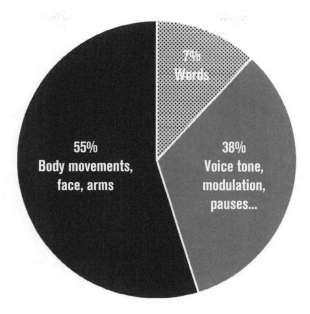

Studying someone's body language alone, without words is like watching a silent movie. During that golden era of filmmaking, an actor had to use facial expressions, gestures, and body signals to communicate with the audience. Physical behavior, the way we hold our stance, move our hands, expressions, and mannerisms all influence non-verbal communication. The face is extremely expressive and can convey a message without saying a word. Each of us can translate the meaning of a frown, smile, scrunched nose, raised eyebrow, or a wink.

A micro-expression is the result of a voluntary and involuntary response occurring simultaneously. They are facial expressions that occur within a fraction of a second; some may be easier to miss than others. Once you know, once you see it, it is hard to un-see the true emotional leakage that occurs regardless of what is being communicated verbally.

MASTERY SKILLS

Master the Seven Universal Micro-Expressions.

Anger	The lips are rolled in tight. The eyes glare and are often squinted. The eyebrows are angled down and pulled together. May flash teeth like a growling dog.	
Happiness	Both lip corners are pulled up toward the tips of the ears versus toward the back of the jaw. You can see the crow's feet around the eyes. Narrowed eye-opening. Cheeks are raised.	
Disgust	The upper lip is pulled up and the nose wrinkled. The eyebrows are pulled down. Sometimes this is seen with just the lips pulled up and apart.	
Sadness *When faking sadness, turning up the inner eyebrows is one of the most difficult movements to make.*	The corners of the lips turn downward. Often the mouth will hang open. The eyes appear heavy, and the inner corners of the eyebrows turn upward. There is a dimpling of the chin.	

Fear	Mouth corners are stretched back toward the jawline. Upper eyelids are wide open. You can literally see the whites of the eyes. Eyebrows are raised and pulled together.	
Surprise *Surprise is the quickest of all emotions and in less than three seconds will turn into one of the other emotions.*	Mouth hangs open. Eyebrows are raised and eyes open wide. Surprise is the briefest of all the universal emotions, its function is to focus our attention on determining what is happening and whether or not it is dangerous.	
Contempt *Contempt is considered the most dangerous of all expressions.*	Lip corner is pulled in and back on one side of face. This is the only emotion demonstrated on one side of the face. It is best characterized as a smirk. The basic notion of contempt is: "I'm better than you and you are lesser than me." The expression of contempt can occur with or without a hint of a smile or angry expression.	

MASTERY SKILLS

Interpret Hand Gestures.

Hand gestures also serve as a substitute for words and can be some of the most obvious body language signals. A thumbs up or thumbs down, a wave or a beckoning motion, all transmit understandable messages. Words and movements occur simultaneously and unconsciously. The words we *choose* to use convey the message we *wish* to communicate, which may not be the same thing our body language is communicating.

Hand gestures have a language of their own. Our brains are hard-wired to engage our hands in accurately communicating our emotions and thoughts.

Open Hands	This a universal behavior of humility, compliance, and cooperation. Also, a sign of "nothing hidden here." Open hands seek trust and honesty.	
Palms Down	Palms down displays are affirmative. It is often used in positions of authority or giving orders. Shows dominance. Think of an officer directing traffic or someone telling you to stop.	
Pointed Finger	A pointed finger is very aggressive. It is also considered rude and makes a person feel lectured. It shows dominance.	

MASTERY SKILLS

Note a Few Other Gestures.

Shoulder Shrugging	This is the classic tell of uncertainty and is the #1 movement we miss. It often reveals what our words do not convey. You'll see this happen on one side or both and often is an indicator of deceit, contradicting what is being said.
Eye Blocking	Eyes closed while speaking is a powerful non-verbal tell of dislike. As if to say "I don't want you to see what I am hiding inside."
Lip Locking	When we disagree with what we see or hear, our lips disappear. Pursed lips are a classic sign of information being suppressed.

DECEPTION DETECTION

Body language is the unspoken element of communication that reveals true emotion and thought. Each gesture or movement can be a valuable key to an emotion a person may be feeling at that time. In the context of agent safety, client *disengagement, deception,* and *stress* signals are the most important nonverbal cues to monitor in the other person's body language. A cluster of disengagement, deception and stress behaviors, brought on by a heightened emotional state, often precedes aggressive conduct.

MASTERY SKILLS

Observe Other Physical Behaviors.

Other discomforting behaviors and their meanings include:

► **Covering the face or rubbing the eyes** = a result of increased tension.

► **Covering the mouth** = uncomfortable with responding or answering the question.

► **Touching the face** = a soothing action. Sometimes it can be a sudden rubbing action on their arm. (*What are they telling you that they feel needs soothing?*)

► **Biting fingernails** = nervous behavior. Also, a soothing action.

► **Clasping the hands**, especially around the head = attempting to hold in or hide their emotions and sometimes accompanied by a holding of the breath.

► **Covering the face** = hiding shame or embarrassment.

► **Pulling in or biting of the lip** = predators understand that this action gives the impression of innocence. You should understand that it can be purposely used to gain your sympathy.

When it comes to your personal safety, the ability to recognize and interpret non-verbal communication when dealing with a predator is one of the most powerful safety tools you have. A physical attack may come suddenly, but there are often warning signs. Before an attack occurs, a predator's physical appearance may change in a way that indicates what is about to happen.

When it comes to your personal safety, the ability to recognize and interpret non-verbal communication when dealing with a predator is one of the most powerful safety tools you have.

MASTERY SKILLS

Look Out for Non-Verbal Pre-Attack Signals.

Facial Skin Sweat—Unless it is 100 degrees or the person is exercising, the face should be relatively dry. In psychological or physiological arousal, sweat gland activity also increases.

If you are showing a home and your buyer exhibits moisture, beading around the temples, or especially above the upper lip, ask yourself why. Does the current situation warrant that sweaty response?

Too much eye contact—There is a myth that liars won't look you in the eye. The truth to that lies more in children than adults. Most deliberate liars will overcompensate, and hold contact for too long.

Face Color–A sudden facial color change, reddening or going pale, may signal intensified emotions of a fight or flight response.

Pulsating Arteries–Anger produces a powerful physiological state of arousal and leads to a rapid surge in blood flow. This is often referred to as the throbbing vein of anger.

Widening Eyes–You can literally see the whites of their eyes. This look is often described as "a deer in headlights" or "flashbulb eyes." This is an involuntary response controlled by emotion and the nervous system. It is a danger sign of an imminent attack.

Rapid Fire Blinking–When the going gets tough, the eyelids get blinking! We blink significantly faster when our nervous system is stressed or aroused.

Breathing–Visible and audible changes in breathing occur when more oxygen is needed to provide the necessary energy to fuel an impending assault.

Fisted Hands–Watch for closed hands and hidden palms. Fisted hands are used when fighting, holding weapons, and concealing them. Watch for hands hidden from your sight, behind the back or in pockets.

Darting Eyes–Scanning the area around you, looking for witnesses and ensuring the attack will go unseen.

Vague Responses or Hesitation in Responses—People aren't generally good at dividing tasks. A predator's mind is on one thing—the attack. They cannot concentrate on answering questions when their minds are focused on the impending assault.

Focused Attention and Targeted Glances—Focused and/or repeated attention on a particular part of the body shows where they will probably strike first.

Thousand-Yard Stare—The person seems to be looking through you. We hear victims state, "He or she was looking at me, but it is as if no-one was there." The predator is mentally shutting down and ready to go on aggressive physical autopilot.

Invading Personal Space—Predators will use various tactics to get close to you or close the gap between you and them, putting you within striking distance.

The upper torso area is a great place to look for clues of an impending attack. There are two primary areas to study. The first is the shoulders. Most people typically stand with a relaxed posture. The shoulders hang in a relaxed way as well. Look for a tense stance that has the shoulders raised higher than usual.

> The upper torso area is a great place to look for clues of an impending attack.

The second place to study is the chest itself. Men and women are different in that most men typically breathe from their stomach, whereas women breathe from their chest. This simply means that when a man breathes, typically, his stomach will move in and out.

Women, on the other hand, will breathe from higher up in their chest. In an attack situation, this role will typically reverse. Be on the lookout for short breaths. If things seem abnormally fidgety, don't overlook the possible message that activity sends.

MASTERY SKILLS

Watch for Hidden Intentions and Self-Ventilating Behavior.

Psychological discomfort, such as heat-rising stress caused by thoughts of an impending attack, will cause distressed ventilating behavior in an effort to cool the sudden rise of body temperature and reduce stress.

Individuals may **run their fingers through their hair** several times in quick succession. Those that wear hats will **lift the hats off their heads** to let in air. Women tend to **lift up the back of the hair** off the nape of the neck. Men tend to **tug at their collar** or **loosen their tie** in an attempt to allow cool air in. Men and women may **tug at the buttons of their shirt** or blouse and pull them forward to allow air in.

MASTERY SKILLS

Be Aware: Feet Are Like Turn Signals.

The feet are the most honest part of the body and hold the secrets to hidden intentions. They are further from the brain and harder to control. The closer together the feet are, the more anxiety a person may be feeling, especially if they are fidgety. **Feet are like a compass and will always point in the direction where they are headed.** When someone intends to leave, at least one foot will be headed in the intended direction. When the feet are pointed toward you, it means that they're not going anywhere else anytime soon.

MASTERY SKILLS

Follow Your Gut Instincts.

Have you ever had a gut feeling or a moment when the hair stood up on the back of your neck and you just *knew*? Your gut instinct is a built-in sensor, an early alarm warning, that is designed to safeguard you. Our subconscious minds constantly evaluate millions of bits of information, conduct a rapid appraisal of the situation, tap into stress, anxiety and fear, and then shoot a message to your brain.

Your gut instincts reflect what your subconscious mind already knows. We then draw on resources within our subconscious mind and instinct kicks in. We tend to want to solve everything logically, and therefore we try to suppress this feeling. In post-attack interviews, victims will often report that they initially had a bad feeling but ignored it, and in retrospect, wish they would have followed their initial feeling.

Listening to your gut instinct could mean the difference between life and death.

Although you may not be able to exactly pinpoint what the danger is, **listening to your gut instinct could mean the difference between life and death.**

WHAT DID SHE MISS?

Let's turn our attention back to the real estate agent attack caught on camera that I shared at the beginning of this chapter. Because the view of this attack is from above, and what is publicly available is such a short clip, we cannot determine some of the body language and micro-expressions discussed in this chapter. However, there are some cues that indicate an impending attack.

We heard the agent tell the predator, "Go! You saw the house. You're done. That's it!" and she turned her attention to her phone. Unless she was dialing 911, her attention should have been on the predator who made her feel uneasy.

While her attention was on her phone, she missed the predator looking straight into the camera. He didn't do this just once, but twice. He was looking at the angle of the camera in an attempt to get the assault out of camera view, so he pushed her backward off the porch and then ran around to the front of the home. There he groped her, not realizing the camera would still catch a partial view.

He also ventilated himself by lifting his hat prior to acting. Mentally incompetent or not, this predator knew exactly what he was about to do to her. The stress of the impending attack on his system caused his body temperature to rise.

He then began to nervously fidget, first with his hat, then with the water bottle as he scanned the area around him. First, he looked to the right and then to the left. He then looked back to the angle of the camera one more time, stepped in closer to the agent, and extended his hand to close the space between himself and the agent, which put her within striking distance.

We cannot quite make out what was being said between the two, but the predator pointed directly at the agent and ventilated once again by lifting his hat. He then pushed the agent off the porch, backward and out of camera view.

Before he actually pushed her, the agent's instincts kicked in, and she can be heard screaming *before* the attack. Did you catch that? Replay the video if you didn't see it.

And did you notice her body language—arms crossed and closed off? With a phone in one hand and her free hand tucked under her opposite arm, she had no defense against this man as he approached to attack.

Most of us will never be face-to-face with a predator, but that doesn't mean that the risk isn't there. Taking proactive steps to stay safe and simply taking some responsibility for your own safety can minimize your chances of being attacked.

Are you the type to run with earbuds in, or turn your attention to your phone while with clients, or read while waiting? In the society we live in today, your situational awareness is essential to narrow the processing time between observation and action.

CHAPTER SEVEN MASTERY SKILLS SUMMARY

1. Master the Seven Universal Micro-Expressions

- ► Anger
- ► Happiness
- ► Disgust
- ► Sadness
- ► Fear
- ► Surprise
- ► Contempt

2. Interpret Hand Gestures

- ► Open Hands
- ► Palms Down
- ► Pointed Finger

3. Note a Few Other Gestures

- ► Shoulder Shrugging
- ► Eye Blocking
- ► Lip Locking

4. Observe Other Physical Behaviors

- ► Covering the face or rubbing the eyes
- ► Covering the mouth
- ► Touching the face
- ► Biting fingernails
- ► Clasping the hands
- ► Covering the face
- ► Pulling in or biting of the lip

5. Look Out for Non-Verbal Pre-Attack Signals

- ▶ Facial Skin Sweat
- ▶ Too much eye contact
- ▶ Face Color
- ▶ Pulsating Arteries
- ▶ Widening Eyes
- ▶ Rapid Fire Blinking
- ▶ Breathing
- ▶ Fisted Hands
- ▶ Darting Eyes
- ▶ Vague Responses or Hesitation in Responses
- ▶ Focused Attention and Targeted Glances
- ▶ Thousand-Yard Stare
- ▶ Invading Personal Space

6. Watch for Hidden Intentions and Self-Ventilating Behavior

- ▶ Individuals may run their fingers through their hair several times in quick succession.
- ▶ Those that wear hats will lift the hats off their heads to let in air.
- ▶ Women tend to lift up the back of the hair off the nape of the neck.
- ▶ Men tend to tug at their collar or loosen their tie in an attempt to allow cool air in.
- ▶ Men and women may tug at the buttons of their shirt or blouse and pull them forward to allow air in.

7. Be Aware: Feet Are Like Turn Signals

► Feet are like a compass and will always point in the direction where they are headed.

8. Follow Your Gut Instincts

► Listening to your gut instinct could mean the difference between life and death.

chapter eight

NEVER ASSUME YOU ARE SAFE

An elderly man didn't like the home he bought, so he
killed his real estate agent. He purchased the home
sight-unseen based on the marketing pictures of the
home. The buyer paid cash, moved in, and called his agent
the following day to tell him he was unhappy with the
purchase and wanted to return the home.

The real estate agent arrived at the home that evening
to discuss options with the elderly man. That is when he
was shot and killed. The buyer called the police to report
the shooting. After police arrived at the home, the buyer,
who answered the door with his gun in his hand, closed
the door, then shot and killed himself.[1]

This scenario begs the question: How much do you
really know about the clients you serve? We share an
important but short period of time with them. For
example, how long has it been since you have had any
dealings with that previous client who is now calling?
The truth is, unless it is a close friend or family member,
we don't get to know them well at all in the short period

we spend with them. We don't stand witness to their day-to-day demeanor. Their financial or family situation may have changed since we last saw them or had a transaction with them. Aspects of people's attitudes and personalities change, sometimes drastically since we've last seen them.

I shared a story with you earlier in the book about a disgruntled client in Michigan who arranged to meet with his real estate agent at the office regarding a home he purchased with the agent's help years before. When the agent joined him in the conference room in his office, the client shot and killed him because he was upset that the market took a dip, and his home was no longer worth the amount he had paid for it.

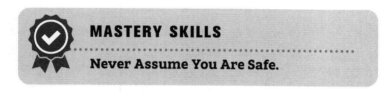

MASTERY SKILLS

Never Assume You Are Safe.

Never let your guard down, even when working with previous clients. We assume it is only strangers who commit crimes, but it can be someone you've worked with several times before, or a friend of a friend, or someone that has been referred to you. Never assume you are safe!

PAY ATTENTION TO YOUR GUT FEELING

To illustrate this point, consider the story of a San Antonio real estate agent. She had received a referral from her husband's best friend, a million-dollar buyer. The husband's friend had been working with him to build a 7-story pharmaceutical building and told the agent that the buyer's funds had been verified—he had billions of dollars. With no reason to question her husband or his best friend, the agent made the arrangements to meet and showed the buyer several properties.

After the showings, the buyer did show interest in one of the homes and wrote an offer with the agent. However, when the agent told him she would need proof of funds to submit the offer, she found it difficult to reach him. When he reappeared a month later, he asked to see two more homes.

On the day of those showings, the buyer called to say his plane was arriving late at the airport. As a result, he would be thirty minutes late to the showing. When the agent arrived at the showing, he was already parked in front of the home. The showing went as planned. He seemed interested but immediately asked to see the second house on the list, the original foreclosure home for which he had already written a contract.

While touring the second home, the agent noticed the buyer walking through much more slowly than at previous showings. She felt something wasn't right and began to feel uncomfortable. Making sure to stay behind him and let him lead the way, she let him go through the bedrooms while she stayed out in the hallway. The buyer then began to question her about what time her bank closed. She assumed he wanted to know what time the area banks closed so he could access funds for a cashier's check for the earnest money before leaving town.

By this time, they had already been in the home for forty-five minutes. Still allowing him to lead the way, they went down the stairs, but when she reached the bottom, the buyer had disappeared elsewhere in the house. The agent's unease about his behavior increased. Her hair stood up on the back of her neck. Something nagged at her not to follow him, so instead she went to the front door, opened it, and waited. After some time passed, the agent yelled out to him that it was getting late and made an excuse on the spot that she had to leave for another appointment.

The buyer walked out from the back part of the house toward her and told her he really wanted to purchase the home. They spoke about updating the offer and needing a cashier's check for the earnest money as they exited the home. After locking the door, the agent bent down to return the key to the lockbox. That's when the buyer attacked her, striking her over the back of her head as hard as he could with a wooden pole that had a metal tip handle.

As he hit her, she fell forward and hit her head on the brick of the home. To the predator's surprise, the agent did not lose consciousness. Instead, she jumped up and confronted the predator, demanding to know why he hit her. The predator told the agent he needed money and demanded $4,000. Right then, the agent knew that not only was he not who everyone told her he was, but also when she had assumed he was asking about her bank hours, his intention all along was to rob her.

The agent reached into her pocket where she had her cell phone and began to try to dial the phone while it was still in her pocket. Just then, a woman passed by on a golf cart. The predator raised the pole at the agent and warned her to be silent, threatening to hit her again. Realizing any cry for help would not be heard over the cart's motor, she complied.

She then tried to reason with her attacker not to kill her, stating she wouldn't tell anyone if he just let her go. She tried to persuade him to get a piece of paper she could sign stating that she had fallen, and he did not attack her. Meanwhile, the agent was still secretly trying to dial numbers on her phone in hopes a call would somehow connect so someone could hear that she was in trouble. Getting more agitated and aggressive, the predator confiscated her phone.

By this time, a UPS truck drove down the street toward them. The agent tried to wave her jacket over her head in hopes of getting the driver's attention, but he didn't see her. When the predator noticed her waving her jacket over her head, she explained that she lifted her jacket to place on her head to stop the bleeding. While she was still trying to convince the predator to let her go, he began to insist she get into his vehicle so he could drive her to the hospital.

The agent, knowing not to get into his vehicle and allow him to take her to a second location, refused to get in. She then saw another car coming their way. She again waved her jacket in the air and turned her head toward the car, thinking if they saw her, they would see the blood gushing from the back of her head and stop to help her. The vehicle's occupants didn't notice and passed them by.

The predator didn't notice the agent's attempt and finally agreed to get a piece of paper for her to write a statement that she had fallen. As he walked to his vehicle, she used the opportunity to try to escape. She could not run to her vehicle because the predator had blocked her in, so she ran into the street with the predator chasing after her. He caught up to her before she could get away, grabbing her by her arm and dragging her back across the street.

Just then, the same car that had passed by moments earlier, circled around and headed back in their direction. This time, when the agent began to scream, the car stopped. Five teenagers piled out of the car to help her. As the teenagers began to yell at the predator to back off and let her go, the predator tried to convince them that it was the real estate agent who attacked and robbed him.

The agent quickly climbed into the car, and the teens took off toward a nearby school where they knew a police officer was on duty. As she was speaking to the police officer, the predator—who attempted to follow them and was circling the area looking for them—pulled up to a stop sign. The police immediately pursued him. When they took him into custody, they found the weapon he used against the agent, along with a 14-inch hunting knife, a rope, and a plat of the subdivision.

The 63-year-old predator, who was living with his parents near where he met the agent, was charged with aggravated assault, and sentenced to sixty years in prison. The agent now has others accompany her when she shows homes and shares her story in hopes that other agents will learn from it.[2]

COMPLACENCY CAN BE DEADLY

We live in a time where big, positive, and long-overdue changes are taking place in our industry. Technology is one reason for those positive changes, but it is a double-edged sword. Technology has also enabled predators to have ready access to information about real estate professionals, allowing them to carefully plan their attacks.

If we are going to make strides in real estate safety, it is going to have to be an all-encompassing, all-hands-on-deck effort starting with individual agents like you and me.

MASTERY SKILLS

Remain Vigilant and Intentional.

Have you ever been so fearful of something that you would not even try it? I'm not talking about dangerously scary things, like jumping off a cliff. Consider public speaking, for instance. So many people are fearful of public speaking that they won't even attempt it. They lack knowledge of how to be successful at it, so instead of learning about it and breaking it down to manageable, achievable steps, they turn their back on it entirely.

In the same context, there is a misconception that ensuring personal safety is laborious, disrupts the potential commission flow, or is too scary to think about. Turning your back on safety doesn't make the problem disappear. Just the opposite. Failing to actively engage in your safety puts you at a disadvantage and a much greater risk. Some agents operate in the hope that nothing bad will happen to them or those around them. By now, we know all too well that blind hope can be a terrible strategy!

Then it happens again—another terrible, preventable,

tragedy. Maybe this time it is in your neck of the woods. Maybe this time it is someone you know. Suddenly everyone is talking about it. There is a sudden outpouring of awareness—for the moment. If our safety awareness were a scale, this close-to-home incident tips the scales to higher awareness and precaution, and therefore lowers the risk.

But then the shock wears off. In almost no time, we grow complacent once again as we get back to the daily grind. The scales tip back in the other direction—awareness level is lower and risk level rises.

In short, we are all willing and anxious to talk about safety only right after something bad happens. We should be more proactive to avoid anything happening in the first place.

MASTERY SKILLS

Talk about Safety Before Tragedy Strikes.

What if we talked about safety *before* tragedy strikes and prevent attacks from happening in the first place? Agents know better than anyone that solutions in real estate begin with communication. I urge you to **start the conversation with those around you.** Ask questions to discover what other agents are implementing in their daily business practice. Take an actionable step toward your safety and remain vigilant and intentional toward your safety as well as those around you.

UNAGI AND SITUATIONAL AWARENESS

My readers who are *Friends* sitcom fanatics will remember the episode where Ross claims to have *unagi*. He claims to possess a situational awareness that he tries to teach Rachel and Phoebe by constantly hiding and jumping out at them when they least expect it. In a similar, but less comical way, if you don't employ unagi (situational awareness), you won't know what to look for—or see a threat heading your way.

> I want you to be self-aware so you can always feel like the seeker, never the hider.

Situational awareness is all about understanding what is going on around you and using that understanding to lead you away from danger. As my own kids were growing up, I taught it to them by saying "be aware of your surroundings," something I still tell them to this day.

Having or acquiring situational awareness can be misunderstood. The term itself is both overused and underutilized. It's not about living in a fearful state; that is exhausting and toxic to our bodies and mind. And I'm not speaking about hyper-vigilance here, either. I'm just asking you to *pay attention to what is going around you.*

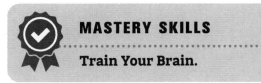

MASTERY SKILLS

Train Your Brain.

Training your brain to be more present and aware can be quite simple and fun. Your reward for doing so is the ability to recognize something that might be a threat to you or others so you can react in time for a quick exit. And it starts at home.

Allow me to get playful here for a minute. Do you remember playing hide-and-seek when you were younger? How did you feel when you were the seeker? Powerful, because you had the upper hand? Adventurous? A discoverer? No fear? How about when you were the hider? Nervous? Panicky? Small? Fearful? I want you to be self-aware so you can always feel like the seeker, never the hider. It is so easy to learn that it won't be long before you don't even recognize you are doing it. Ready?

MASTERY SKILLS

Think Hide-and-Seek.

Instead of going home and unlocking the door, dropping your belongings, and throwing your keys off to the side, stop right where you are and launch the seeker in you. Ask yourself:

- ► If I were to hide, where would I hide?
- ► If I were to jump out at someone from somewhere, where would that place be?
- ► If I had to grab something to protect myself, what would that be?
- ► How would I get to that protection?
- ► Where are my exits?

You will have a better awareness when arriving at a dark home by knowing where to look so you are not caught off-guard. Just like an Olympic athlete mentally rehearsing a routine for success, you can prepare your mind for action.

MASTERY SKILLS

Become the Seeker.

The next time you enter a new space, or the next time you have an open house, be a seeker. Explore the home, take stock of what you have at your disposal to protect yourself, and find your exits. If a threat comes your way, you'll be able to react faster. Your brain will automatically know what to do because you've already mapped it out in your head, just as if you have been through it before.

> Just like an Olympic athlete mentally rehearsing a routine for success, you can prepare your mind for action.

When my kids were younger, we would go to the theater. As soon as we found our seats, I'd tell them to look for the exits. Once all the exits were located, they had to locate the closest one to us. After they identified it, I'd have them count how many rows of seats there were until they reached the exit. Then, when they knew how many rows of seats there were, I told them that if anything happened and the lights went out or something obstructed their view, they now knew how many seats on the end of the rows they had to touch until they reached the exit.

It was a game to them. I am sure everyone around us thought I was trying to keep their attention until the event started, but I was actually teaching them safety at a young age so they would not be scared. In fact, when we would leave, they would touch each seat and count them on their way out. What did that do? It prepared their minds to react so if anything happened, they knew exactly what to do. It would feel natural for them because they had already rehearsed it in their mind so many times that it became automatic. When we do that, our brains assume we've already done it before, so it is no longer unknown.

KEEPING YOUR BACK TO THE WALL

My nephew, Nick, has always known that he was going to dedicate his life to serving the public. He joined an Explorer program in the 17th District in Chicago at the age of seven, so it seems as if he has been on the police force his entire life. When we met for lunch one day, the waitress sat us at a table in the middle of the restaurant. She asked, "Is this table okay?"

To my surprise, my well-mannered nephew refused it. He pointed to another table and respectfully asked if we could be seated at that table. I didn't question it. When we walked over to the table, trying to be considerate, I made my way to the back of the table so those following me wouldn't have to maneuver around me to get to their seats. As I did, my nephew asked me to sit in a different seat at the table. Again, I didn't question it.

Once we were seated and the waitress left, I questioned it. I believe my exact words were "What the heck, dude? What is with the musical chairs?" He went on to explain that he wanted his back against a wall so he could not be surprised by someone coming up behind him. He went on to explain that his seat was in a place where he had the perfect view of what was going on around us—situational awareness. Was he paranoid? Absolutely not. Was he prepared to react if anything went awry? He absolutely was.

Why do I share this with you? So you can take this information with you to your next open house.

MASTERY SKILLS
Keep Your Back to the Wall.

Position yourself so your back is against the wall if seated and have an open view and an awareness of what is going on around you. This way you'll be better prepared to act if necessary.

MASTERY SKILLS
Stay More Alert All Day, Every Day, in Every Situation.

While walking your own neighborhood or through your town, at a party or a restaurant, you might discover things right under your nose that you never paid any attention to before by staying alert.

As you build your situational awareness, when you enter a new space, make a point to notice the people around you and their behavior. Pay attention to anything that can lead to a negative outcome. Pay attention to objects that can become a weapon or an obstacle. Know your exit points.

MASTERY SKILLS

Watch Your Transition Zones.

Transition zones are places we must pass through when getting from one place to another. They can include the entrance when we are getting the key from the lockbox or unlocking the front door. They can also include the stairway when moving through a home. It may be the path between you, the house, your car and your freedom, or the parking lot after an event. Whenever we are moving from one space to another, these transition zones present possible attack points.

MASTERY SKILLS

Never Check Out while You Are Out.

Keep your awareness heightened and remain in the present. The time to let your brain check out and think about the showing you just had or are about to have, or how much fun the party was and texting others, is when you are back at home or the office. Pay attention to your surroundings. By paying attention to your environment, you'll see any threats, long before they see you.

MASTERY SKILLS

Stay Travel Aware.

So many real estate agents travel. A friend told me a story one day that changed the way I travel. Her friend had entered her locked hotel room only to see a pair of feet of someone hiding behind the curtains. As she ran from the room screaming, he ran out of the room behind her and disappeared into the hotel. Apparently, he had been able to enter the room earlier as the door was closing when the maid had turned her back.

When traveling to conferences or on vacation, I become a seeker! When entering a hotel room, I'll open the closet and bathroom doors, pull back the curtains and then pull up the sides of the bedding to look under the bed. I have never found a hotel bed that isn't on a platform with no possibility of hiding under it, but it hasn't stopped me from looking anyway, always seeking and being prepared to act, adapt, or make decisions in a changing environment.

STOP BEING SO NICE

One of the most valuable tools you have in your possession right now is your intuition or instincts. We are born with instincts to help us survive. However, when our instincts shout out to us, we tend to stall them or even worse, override them and quiet them down.

MASTERY SKILLS

Don't Get Caught Up in Political Politeness.

As real estate professionals, we can be too polite sometimes to ensure we don't offend anyone. Even if our warning signs are blaring like a tornado siren, causing our hearts to pound a little faster and our breathing rate to increase, we may question if we are overreacting. Even as we move slower and sometimes even freeze because our hair stands on end, we may still enter into a negotiation with ourselves.

Some judge this intuition to be a feeling resulting from a personal judgment. *Maybe it is just her personality to invade my space*, or, *Maybe he didn't mean anything by that remark.* But know this: **Your intuition, natural instincts, or gut feeling will not form a protective opinion based on perceived social status or looks**. If you need to ask yourself anything, ask yourself, *Is this a message I formed in my own head, or is this a message coming from the core of my being?*

> Safety is a right and responsibility that never requires permission.

The more you cultivate the awareness of your own intuition, the more you'll learn to trust it. The more you trust it, the more willing you will be to protect yourself rather than being worried about hurting someone's feelings or offending someone.

Politeness is a courtesy, but safety is a right and responsibility that never requires permission.

BE ALERT TO STALKING BEHAVIOR

A male real estate agent was conducting an open house when two men entered, describing themselves as father and son. As the son captured the attention of the agent by engaging in conversation, the father wandered through the home. The agent felt suspicious of the pair but couldn't quite put his finger on why. Was he overreacting? Were they there to *case* the home and return later to burglarize it? They just didn't feel like normal buyers to him.

Not being able to shake the uneasy feeling he was experiencing, the agent went upstairs to find the father standing in one of the bedrooms, staring at a wall that held school certificates and pictures of the children that lived in the home. Noticing the odd behavior of how much attention was given to what was hanging on walls, the agent quickly asked the man if he could help with anything. The man commented that it was a nice home and proceeded to leave.

The agent felt the man was looking for information on a person inside the home, although it didn't make much sense to him. When he later discussed the father-son duo with the seller, she immediately knew that it was her estranged father that had come through her house. She explained that she had been hiding from him for fifteen years. Little did she know, her father had hired a private investigator who gave him her and her husband's name and their address.

Days later, the man showed up at the kids' school, hiding behind a tree as she dropped them off. He slid letters under her door at her home and threatened her, saying she was being watched. She sought police protection and filed for an emergency protection order against him as she had to do years prior. She finally fled overseas with her husband and kids to escape him.

A few years later, she would see the man—who was also estranged from his ex-wife and other children—in the news. He had once again hired a private investigator to find his other children, also in hiding. This time the investigator followed the family and was able to give the estranged father his youngest daughter's train schedule. As the young girl left the train and walked home, she unknowingly led the man directly to the home where they were hiding. The father entered the home where he shot and killed his 15-year-old son and 13-year-old daughter as they hid under a desk. The boy's body was found over his sister's as he tried to shield her from the bullets. The murders were the culmination of a decades-long history of domestic violence inflicted on a total of seven ex-partners and ten children.

The real estate agent who acted on his instincts and alerted his seller of a peculiar incident may have prevented another tragedy from occurring. The estranged father was never held responsible for his actions. After killing the teenagers, he went home and killed himself. The mom, who wasn't home at the time of the killings, could not cope with the tragedy of her kids being killed and took her own life.[3]

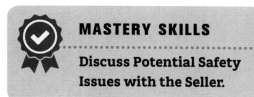

MASTERY SKILLS

Discuss Potential Safety Issues with the Seller.

No matter the situation, it is important to practice safety protocols. When hosting open houses, it may be prudent to ask if there is anyone the agent should be aware of or anyone the seller might not want through their home.

FACED WITH DANGER

Now that you understand situational awareness, let me just add that life and death are not a game of hide-and-seek. You've learned how to cultivate and activate your situational awareness in any new space you enter, but if the building catches fire, you would not hide and hope the fire doesn't find you. You would hopefully get the hell out of there and run as fast and as far as you could from it until you could call 911.

A predator is just as unpredictable as a fire.

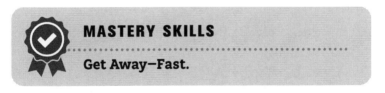

MASTERY SKILLS

Get Away—Fast.

The goal is to always **put as much time and distance you can between you and the predator.**

MASTERING YOUR FEAR RESPONSE

Imagine driving down an expressway. Suddenly, the car next to you starts to lose control, swerving back and forth toward your lane. How might you respond? You could let it happen and not remove yourself from the threat or danger. You could quickly brake. Or you could accelerate or move over to the next lane to avoid a collision and remove yourself from the danger. This sudden threatening situation does not provide enough time to sit and decide what to do; you just respond and react instinctively without even thinking about it until it is over.

This is an example of your freeze-flight-fight response to danger, another built-in automatic defense system we all possess. The perception or act of a threat activates our sympathetic nervous system and triggers a response that prepares the body to freeze, flight, or fight. For example, when you hear someone yell, "Look Out!" you might be surprised to learn just how fast you can move! It's a natural response, not a conscious one—you don't get to choose. You're born with this self-protective instinct.

Mastering and understanding our fear response is critical to our survival from a threat or danger. Everyone reacts differently. Because our fear responses happen automatically, we are typically not actively deciding which response is most effective in a given situation. Our brain is signaling our body to get ready to react and react fast. If you have never been through a traumatic experience, you might not know how your body will respond.

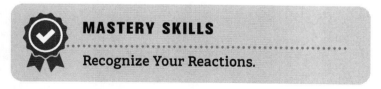

MASTERY SKILLS

Recognize Your Reactions.

Recognizing and mastering our instantaneous reaction, when it happens, may help you escape safely from a dangerous situation.

FREEZE—Nearly everyone freezes. The question is for how long? Some freeze for just a fraction of a second, while others may stay in that state for far too long. In a split second, the brain decides that we cannot take on the threat or flee from it, so instead, the best way to survive what is happening is to freeze. During the freeze state, some may experience a hyper sense of focus (tunnel vision) and move on to the next state (fight or flight) while others experience a completely frozen state, unable to move. If you recognize you are in a frozen state, you can break it by mustering the strength to command your focus to the present. Recognize it, command yourself to GET UP, GET MOVING and GET OUT! Redirect the freeze state and focus on what you have to do to get to safety.

FLIGHT—This is running away and escaping the threat. Put as much time and distance between you and the threat as possible. Sometimes that means just out of arm's reach, using barriers like a kitchen island, until you have the opportunity to get further away. Flight should always be our first goal and our end goal, even when it cannot be our first response!

FIGHT—It's important to recognize that some threats may leave us with no other option but to fight for our life. We might not see an attack before it happens, but make up your mind right now, not only will you fight back, but you will act forcefully and decisively. You are stronger than you think. You have an extra reserve strength tank that you don't even know exists. If you get tired of fighting for yourself, pull up your reserves and fight for those who are waiting for you back at home.

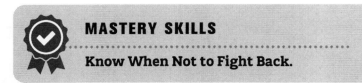

MASTERY SKILLS

Know When Not to Fight Back.

The only time to be submissive is when being robbed. Give the mugger what he wants. Yes, giving up your personal belongings just because someone else feels entitled to them stings, but that sting hurts far less than fighting for your life.

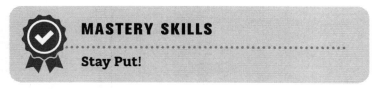

MASTERY SKILLS

Stay Put!

Never let a predator take you to a second location. There is absolutely nothing that is going to get any better for you at a second location. It only gets worse. Do anything and everything in your power to keep from being taken to a second location!

O.O.D.A.

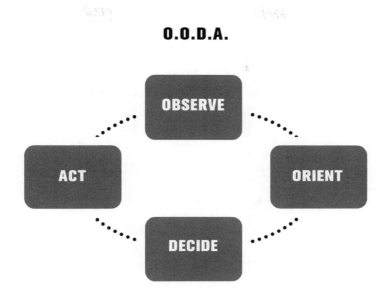

Source: Colonel John Boyd

The OODA (Observe, Orient, Decide, Act) loop is a process we go through hundreds of times in a single day. It is what happens between a situation and a decision. How fast is your OODA loop? That depends on you.

There are two factors that can affect your reaction time during the Orient stage. They are denial—when you *refuse* to accept the event is happening to you—and an emotional reaction that causes a filter or cloud to haze over your critical thinking skills. You *wish* this wasn't happening to you. "Oh man, please don't let this be happening." Both factors can and will affect your reaction time. But you can overcome this with training. Let's take a brief look at how we work through the four stages of the loop.

- **OBSERVE**—Observation of unfolding circumstances. Situational awareness. Gathering information quickly using sight, sound, intuition, etc.

- **ORIENT**—Making sense of the information we observed. Coming to terms with the new circumstances you are in. Placing your observations into proper context.

- **DECIDE**—What are your options? Being prepared and having a willingness to act.

- **ACT**—Implement your decision and take action.

OODA acts as a bridge that connects situational awareness to action. We often unconsciously follow the OODA pattern in any decision we make by moving through the four stages of the loop. It is important to note that in a dangerous situation, we utilize OODA over and over again as we progress through the threat until we reach safety.

For example, my bank has four locations in my town alone. The closest one to me has an ATM that is located behind the bank, far away from the street view, surrounded by an acre of woods. It is in the most terrible location possible for any consumer. I try to make it there during the day when needed, but sometimes I'm forced to go after dark. Even at 4:30 in Chicago, if it is winter, it is pitch black outside! This is the OODA loop I run in my mind:

- **Observation**—I am about to use the ATM in the dark, behind a building and out of view, next to the woods. This can be a place of hidden danger.

- **Orient**—It is super dark back here. I need to be in heightened situational awareness. It doesn't look like anyone else is around.

- **Decision**—I am going to remain focused and aware of my surroundings. I keep checking my mirrors, and at any sight of suspicious activity, I'm out of here!

- **Action**—I retrieve my money through the ATM then get out of there and to the street side before I even have the chance to roll up my window all the way.

If you see something suspicious, or the threat continues, you run the OODA loop again until you are safe:

- **Observation**—When I arrive at the ATM, there are two people sitting in the back parking lot.

- **Orient**—The bank is closed; there is no good reason for them to be there. I focus on their whereabouts at all times.

- **Decide**—I decide it is best to not utilize the ATM at that time.

- **Act**—I don't stop, and instead, I get out of there, driving to the other side of town to a well-lit ATM.

MASTERY SKILLS

Understand and Practice OODA.

We can accelerate our reaction time by moving through the pattern or process consciously. And by practicing conscious OODA, we are less likely to explain away or deny a potential warning sign. It will also help those that have a hard time with being decisive and getting caught between the first two stages, Observation and Orient, endlessly looping without making a decision and taking action which can result in a less favorable outcome. Think of a squirrel that runs back and forth in front of your car trying to decide if it will cross the street.

Consciously progressing through the OODA loop, practicing in our minds, will help to protect you from getting stuck by recognizing where you get stuck and forcing yourself to decide and act. Acting quickly, effectively changes the condition of the circumstances you are in and could mean the difference in getting you out of an unwanted situation.

SAFETY AND SECURITY FOR YOUR INTERCONNECTED WORLD

Personal harm is not the only crime that the real estate industry faces. We have all heard of the wire transfer that was intercepted by hackers or malware that has taken over a computer network because someone mistakenly clicked on the wrong link. Real estate professionals collect a considerable amount of data, not only on transactions, but also on the parties to those transactions. And it makes us a target. Significant data requires substantial protection!

MASTERY SKILLS

Throw a Wide Safety Net.

Agent safety must extend to safety and security for our clients, whether that be protecting confidential information or securing valuables and the home itself during showings. The way real estate professionals handle client data and security not only instills trust but can also become a competitive business advantage.

CHAPTER EIGHT MASTERY SKILLS SUMMARY

1. **Never Assume You Are Safe**

    ► Never let your guard down.

2. **Remain Vigilant and Intentional**

3. **Talk about Safety Before Tragedy Strikes**

    ► Start the conversation with those around you.

4. **Train Your Brain**

5. **Think Hide-and-Seek**

6. **Become the Seeker**

7. **Keep Your Back to the Wall**

8. **Stay More Alert All Day, Every Day, in Every Situation**

9. **Watch Your Transition Zones**

10. **Never Check Out while You Are Out**

11. **Stay Travel Aware**

12. **Don't Get Caught Up in Political Politeness**

   ► Your intuition, natural instincts, or gut feeling will not form a protective opinion based on perceived social status or looks.

13. **Discuss Potential Safety Issues with the Seller**

14. **Get Away—Fast.**

   ► Put as much time and distance you can between you and the predator.

15. **Recognize Your Reactions**

   ► Freeze
   ► Flight
   ► Fight

16. **Know When Not to Fight Back.**

17. **Stay Put!**

18. Understand and Practice OODA

- ► Observe
- ► Orient
- ► Decide
- ► Act

19. Throw a Wide Safety Net

chapter nine

YOUR SAFETY, YOUR RESPONSIBILITY

I have heard it said that a safety culture in an organization starts at the top. But does safety awareness and practice really flow from the top down, or does it start with the people on the front lines? The truth is building and maintaining a successful safety culture is an evolving process that requires a commitment from *everyone* at *all levels* of any organization. The culture is created by shared beliefs, attitudes, and practices. Collaboration at all levels is critical to prevent lasting harm.

> The experiences and wisdom acquired from days gone by can be utilized as a springboard to the future.

Let's start at the brokerage level. Something unique to the real estate industry is the designated managing broker supervisory rule. State statutes mandate brokers to exercise supervision over their agents. A safety culture can be a significant asset or a tremendous liability. Innovation, growth, and development in terms of agent safety cannot occur by pretending we still live in a world that long ago passed us by. We can't address today's challenges with yesterday's thinking.

However, history does provide us with a framework of knowledge. The experiences and wisdom acquired from days gone by can be utilized as a springboard to the future.

MASTERY SKILLS

Incorporate a Safety Policy.

If you haven't done so already, there is an opportunity here to transform safety insights into valuable actions by incorporating a safety plan or policy at your local office. Ask questions such as:

► What policies do you have in place for your door-keeper or receptionist, the first person a visitor interacts with?

► How would the receptionist alert others in the office of any potential threats?

► How are visitors announced?

► Do you have a visitor log book policy?

► Are security cameras in place in public areas of the office?

► What safety policies do you have for working in the office alone or after hours?

► Are those who are licensed to conceal and carry allowed to bring weapons onto the premises?

► What is the process for reporting a concern?

► What about active shooter office training?

► Do your employees and agents know what to do and where to go?

Police departments nationwide need offices just like yours to train their policemen and women in active shooter situations. By partnering with your local department, not only are you providing necessary training for your staff and agents, but you also benefit because that same police department may one day be responding to your call for help and already know the layout of your office.

MASTERY SKILLS

Incorporate Agent Safety into Your Weekly Meetings.

Let your agents know you care about their well-being. Fill that blank space of agents not knowing what they don't know. Bring your agents into the conversation by picking one of the Mastery Skills outlined in this book to talk about at your weekly meetings. Encourage discussion and provide safety training to mitigate your risks and liabilities by implementing an office safety culture.

MASTERY SKILLS

Create a Safety Committee.

Local Associations provide unique member benefits, business tools, education, and resources on a local level for brokerages and agents.

The importance of establishing an association safety committee is emphasized by the negatives of *not* having one. Safety committees can have a significant impact and play a key role in the safety of their members by providing personal protection education, the latest area safety information, and other tools and resources. As far as safety incidents go, the local association is going to be one of the first to be alerted in an agent safety incident.

MASTERY SKILLS

Make a Plan.

Implementing a crisis communication plan is essential for the protection of others. When a safety emergency occurs, the need to communicate facts is immediate. Effective alerts include enough detailed information so agents understand the proper protective actions to take to reduce their risk.

State and national associations also provide unique member benefits, business tools, education, and resources to their members, which includes local associations and brokerages. Each hosts special safety committees, articles, videos, webinars, grants for further education, and resources to better understand the potential risks, in addition to a safety network at the state and national level.

MASTERY SKILLS

Make Safety a Core Value.

All associations and brokerages have strategic priorities. Safety should not be a stand-alone strategy. The development of an effective safety culture requires a participative approach that includes agents, brokerages, management, and associations. Safety must remain an integral part of the overall operational plan.

You do not need a policy to be enacted by anyone to protect yourself.

Instead of designating safety as a strategic priority, consider it a *core value*. While an organization's strategic plan may change from time to time, its core values do not.

You may or may not have much of a voice in what policies and procedures are put in place at your brokerage office. However, you don't need to wait for the higher-ups. You do not need a policy to be enacted by *anyone* to protect yourself. As a real estate agent, you are an independent contractor, the boss, manager, CEO, CFO, and CXO of your own business.

MASTERY SKILLS

Take Ownership of Your Safety.

In fact, as an independent contractor, I would argue you *are* the top! The *contractor* part of that term means you aligned yourself with, have a written agreement with, or executed a contract with a brokerage. While you may have separate policies, rules, and regulations to follow with them, you still manage your own business. Don't wait for safety tips to fall into your lap via a memo. You are in charge of you. You must build safety precautions for your own safety.

> Don't wait for safety tips to fall into your lap via a memo. You are in charge of you. You must build safety precautions for your own safety.

This book, and the *Mastery Skills of Safe Practices for Real Estate Professionals* accompaniment, will provide you the tools you need to get started.

A SPECIAL NOTE ABOUT CYBER SECURITY CONCERNS

In addition to personal safety, real estate agents are charged with the security of client information. With more and more transaction details conducted online and with client data stored online, the industry has become vulnerable to cybercriminals.[1]

MASTERY SKILLS

Guard Your Cyberspace!

According to the FBI's Internet Crime Complaint Center, there were a record number of complaints in 2020: 791,790, with reported losses exceeding $4.1 billion—a 69% increase in total complaints from 2019.

Business E-mail Compromise (BEC) schemes continued to be the costliest: 19,369 complaints with an adjusted loss of approximately $1.8 billion. Phishing scams were also prominent: 241,342 complaints, with adjusted losses of over $54 million.

The number of ransomware incidents also continues to rise, with 2,474 incidents reported in 2020. There were more than 13,000 victims of real estate cybercrime in 2020, resulting in total losses of $213 million.

The cyber-attack most real estate professionals are familiar with is the BEC, a sophisticated phishing scam. In this crime, the attacker relies upon the ability to look like a trusted partner. They send instructions to wire funds for a transaction to a fraudulent account.

According to the 2021 Wire Fraud and Cyber Crime Survey conducted by the American Land Title Association, title insurance professionals reported attempted fraud in a third of all real estate and mortgage transactions.[2] *One in three!*

Cybercriminals have broadened their scope to attack other players in the field, too, including agents, buyers, inspectors, insurance agents, title companies, attorneys, etc. It's not just BEC scams that are being committed against real estate businesses; others include ransomware, malicious attachments, and attacks on cloud-based services. Cybercriminals also target cell phones.

MASTERY SKILLS

Beef Up Your Cyber Strategy!

Protecting your real estate business starts with a cybersecurity strategy. It is the responsibility of brokerages and agents to safeguard their clients' confidential information and implement data security measures. Make sure all internet-enabled devices have the latest operating systems, browsers, and security software. This includes mobile devices that access your wireless network.

Data breaches usually all start with one thing in common: human error. Regular cybersecurity awareness training for your staff and agents is another critical safety measure to include in your strategy.

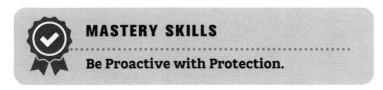

MASTERY SKILLS

Be Proactive with Protection.

Below are some key steps to protecting your computer from intrusion:[3]

► **Keep Your Firewall Turned On.** A firewall helps protect your computer from hackers who might try to gain access to crash it, delete information, or even steal passwords or other sensitive information. Software firewalls are widely recommended for single computers. The software is prepackaged on some operating systems or can be purchased for individual computers. For multiple networked computers, hardware routers typically provide firewall protection.

► **Install or Update Your Antivirus Software.** This software is designed to prevent malicious programs from embedding on your computer. If it detects malicious code, like a virus or a worm, it works to disarm or remove it. Viruses can infect computers without users' knowledge. Most types of antivirus software can be set up to update automatically.

► **Install or Update Your Antispyware Technology.** Spyware is just what it sounds like—software that is surreptitiously installed on your computer to let others peer into your activities on the computer. Some spyware collects information about you without your consent or produces unwanted pop-up ads on your web browser. Some operating systems offer free spyware protection, and inexpensive software is readily available for download on the Internet or at your local computer store. Be wary of ads on the Internet offering downloadable antispyware—in some cases, these products may be fake and may actually contain spyware or other malicious code.

► **Keep Your Operating System Up-to-Date.** Computer operating systems are periodically updated to stay in tune with technology requirements and to fix security holes. Be sure to install the updates to ensure your computer has the latest protection.

► **Be Careful What You Download.** Carelessly downloading email attachments can circumvent even the most vigilant anti-virus software. Never open an e-mail attachment from someone you don't know and be wary of forwarded attachments from people you do know. They may have unwittingly advanced malicious code.

► **Turn Off Your Computer.** With the growth of high-speed Internet connections, many opt to leave their computers on and ready for action. The downside is that being "always-on" renders computers more susceptible. Beyond firewall protection, which is designed to fend off unwanted attacks, turning the computer off effectively severs an attacker's connection—be it spyware or a botnet that employs your computer's resources to reach out to other unwitting users.

► **Contact Your FBI Field Office.** If you or your organization is the victim of a network intrusion, data breach, or ransomware attack, contact your nearest FBI field office or report it at tips.fbi.gov.

ONWARD AND UPWARD

Real estate professionals compete against other real estate professionals for business, focusing on their strengths and what sets them apart from the others—the competitive edge.

MASTERY SKILLS

Distinguish Yourself with Your Safety Protocols.

Make safety part of your listing presentations, buyer consultations, and new agent onboarding. Talk about the steps you take for seller safety, from pre-screening buyers and agents who enter their homes, to safeguarding personal belongings and securing personal information.

Make your buyer aware that you are familiar with the latest phishing and wire fraud cyber-crimes and the steps you take to ensure your system is safe in protecting their private information. Let them know *you* will communicate with them every step of their journey and especially that important sensitive information, like wiring instructions, will be done *in person* and never by email.

Finally, when interviewing new potential agents, make sure to talk about your office safety culture. Company policies, agent training, tools, and resources you provide not only make an agent aware of the challenges professionals face in the field today, but prepares them for action if they find themselves in a risky situation. It may just be that one competitive edge that sets you apart from the rest.

CHANGE MUST BE OUR CONSTANT

The challenges we face with safety in the real estate industry are great, but the opportunity to stimulate innovation in protective measures and solutions is even greater. The assault cases throughout this book explored and exploited multiple overlapping factors that were preventable with industry-wide safety training.

We have identified the need for changes to the way we conduct business. The lessons we have learned should lead to solutions, fresh approaches, and new commitments. It will take an evolving effort with the engagement of all to effect fundamental, prevention-focused change.

How do we move forward with the challenges of uncertainty? Through adaptive business practices. We live, work, and play in a world that is changing right before our eyes. Committing to constant growth, adaptive practices, and systems for continuous improvement ensures your business and your safety will bridge challenging waters.

To safely unlock our future in this industry requires us to adopt change as expectations and behaviors in this world also change. Instituting safety processes requires changes in attitudes, beliefs, and behaviors. When faced with an overwhelming turn of events, it's not okay to say, *I just can't think about all of this right now.* While you might need time to work through what's happened and adapt to new circumstances, it's important to recognize that ignoring it won't change the reality of the situation.

If you don't adopt safety training, practices, and strategies in your daily business practice, you cannot expect to benefit from them when you need them the most.

CHAPTER NINE MASTERY SKILLS SUMMARY

1. **Incorporate a Safety Policy**

2. **Incorporate Agent Safety into Your Weekly Meetings**

3. **Create a Safety Committee**

4. **Make a Plan**

5. **Make Safety a Core Value**

6. **Take Ownership of Your Safety**

7. **Guard Your Cyberspace!**

8. **Beef Up Your Cyber Strategy!**

9. **Be Proactive with Protection**

   - ► Keep your firewall turned on.
   - ► Install or update your antivirus software.
   - ► Install or update your antispyware technology.
   - ► Keep your operating system up-to-date.
   - ► Be careful what you download.
   - ► Turn off your computer.
   - ► Contact your FBI field office.

10. **Distinguish Yourself with Your Safety Protocols**

    - ► Make safety part of your listing presentations, buyer consultations, and new agent onboarding.

THE GOOD, THE BAD, THE UGLY: REWRITING THE STORY

"If violent crime is to be curbed, it is only the intended victim who can do it. The felon does not fear the police, and he fears neither judge nor jury. Therefore, what he must be taught to fear is his victim."

—JEFF COOPER

Violent attacks don't happen at random. Responsibility for real estate agent assault always lies with the predator. Responsibility for both individual and collective agent safety lies with the real estate professional(s). Implementing even a few of the mastery skills throughout this book places you in the position of becoming a difficult target with the power and the capability to stop a predator in their tracks and avoid becoming a victim.

You are in control of your risk settings, the ones that affect your day-to-day life and help create a safer environment for you and your family. Accessibility, due diligence, behavioral cues, statement analysis and situational awareness are all important elements of the safety prevention equation.

A solution blueprint has been laid out throughout the previous chapters. It acts as a bridge that aids in preventing and deterring a violent encounter and helps to get you safely to the other side.

Whether you know it or not, you have been studying facial expressions, body language and vocal tones since the day you were born.

It is nearly impossible for anyone to act without giving some sort of body language clue that signals their intention. The most unfortunate warning signs are those that are sent and received but somehow missed before tragedy occurs. When it comes to agent safety, nothing is more important than being able to foresee violent behavior headed our way.

Real estate professionals are naturally driven to perform at high levels. Sometimes that can lead to ignoring harmful practices due to a belief that tragedy only strikes elsewhere. It could lead to shortcutting safety to save time or to facilitate a potential sale, ignoring the potential long-term consequences of their actions.

Willful blindness or denial is a coping mechanism that has a dark side. Refusing to acknowledge that something is wrong is one way of coping with emotional conflict, stress, and threatening information, but it doesn't change the reality of the situation.

You are a master! Each of us was born with the ability to communicate without words. Whether you know it or not, you have been studying facial expressions, body language and vocal tones since the day you were born.

A baby knows how to get what it wants without saying a word. A parent can tell the difference in the needs of a baby by a difference in a cry just as a baby can recognize a happy face when they see one.

You watch others as they are talking, unconsciously noticing and interpreting their facial expressions and their hand gestures. You understand their vocal tone when they speak. We may ask "Are you okay?" and although they reply with a yes, we know better because we notice their sunken demeanor, sad eyes, or low tone.

The unknown can be scary. Don't overthink it. We cannot live in a state of panic. The real estate industry evolves and changes all the time. Simply embrace the necessary changes you need to make to conduct business safely and take 100% responsibility for doing that. Don't leave it up to anyone else.

Although you might not have much experience with coming face-to-face with danger, you now have the tools and knowledge to master dangerous situations. Have a little fun practicing some of the exercises in this book with agents in your office.

Taking control of our safety means learning from past events and rewriting our story going forward. May the mastery you gained keep you safe and out of harm's way.

Kelly Simpson is an internationally-recognized real estate safety expert with over two decades of experience in the real estate industry. She is an active REALTOR® with real-world experience in the diverse challenges real estate professionals face today.

Kelly is Master Certified in Body Language with an exceptional record of success in protective intelligence, policy authorship, and the assessment and vulnerability reduction of threats in the real estate industry. She has extensive training in the use of verbal and physical cues plus voice and statement analysis to detect deception and dangerous personalities.

She has delivered public and private presentations to global audiences, including *The Oprah Winfrey Show*, offering a blend of hard skills training, business savvy, and strategic insight.

Kelly is the founder and CEO of the National Safety Council of Real Estate (NSCORE), a premiere threat management organization dedicated to real estate professionals, brokerages, and associations, providing expert consultation, resources, training, and protective strategies for staying safe.

For more information, or to contact Kelly Simpson, visit NSCORE.org

acknowledgements

Writing a book is no easy task and much more difficult than I could have ever imagined, especially when writing about such senseless tragedy that just shakes me to my core. I've heard actors state that sometimes while rehearsing for a role when filming a movie, they lose themselves and find it difficult to get out of character. While writing this book, I could feel the deceit and tragedy these innocent real estate professionals endured, as if I was right there with them. There were many times that I was so mentally shaken, I had to get up and walk away. Only these weren't actors rehearsing or filming a movie. They are innocent victims who didn't get the chance to simply walk away. And it was for that reason I could come back to sharing their stories and the message of agent safety.

I would like to express sincere appreciation to all the courageous agents and their families who have shared and continue to share their stories of tragedy and deception with hopes of protecting others from future senseless acts. And my deepest condolences to the lives lost and those families who have lost loved ones in the burgeoning acts of senseless tragedies committed against real estate professionals. Throughout history, the real estate family has always risen to meet challenges with decisive action, inspiring innovation and remarkable determination. Together we can stand up to the forces of evil and prevail.

A special thank you to Carl Carter, Jr. and the Beverly Carter Foundation for being a beacon of light in darkness, shining the spotlight on such a critical issue in the real estate industry and inspiring positive change in agents' lives. Thank you, Carl, for sharing your beautiful momma with us, your quick wit, making us laugh while we learn, empowering us to want to do more, and for the journal that called out to me every day and inspired this book.

To NAR and each state and local association who have recognized the need for safety committees and task forces, and the members who so tirelessly volunteer and dedicate their time to agent safety education, thank you for your outstanding service! Your hard work does not fall on deaf ears. WE HEAR YOU! WE APPRECIATE YOU!

A special thank you to those who have been in the audiences of my interactive presentations and training programs over the past few years, to the clients who have invited me to serve those audiences, and to the agents who have been trailblazers in agent safety mastery as well as those who are just acknowledging that there is more we can do. You have shown such an inspiring thirst for new tools and practices that look beyond the obvious and explore significant opportunity in pursuing a shared mastery plan that bridges our past, present, and future, while keeping each other safe and out of harm's way. Thank you for putting faith in me to drive you to look at safety through renewed senses. You also inspired me to write this book.

I'd like to express my admiration, respect, and appreciation to Bill Blankschaen, Akemi Cole and Jen Truitt for the many months of crafting, editing my vision, and for helping me to process the years of heartache that I carried with me for our industry and fellow agents. For listening so intently to the struggle before us, for caring so deeply about the message that needed to be shared and for pulling it out of me. Thank you for your outstanding guidance, for your continued support, new friendships, and giving so much of yourselves to a dedicated cause.

Sometimes God places people in your life, and together you have a higher calling. This book would have never been possible if it wasn't for one of my brilliant mentors, Janine Driver. An unlikely meeting that led to a friendship, I am eternally grateful to personally know such a wonderful human, a giving angel, and caring of people everywhere. Janine, you have so generously invited me in and taught me so much more than I could have ever imagined. Thank you for sharing your life's purpose in making our world a better place!

I am also eternally grateful and deeply honored that we have with us Adorna Carroll and her invaluable contributions and insight in writing the foreword of *Not Today, Predator!* Adorna is universally known as a beacon of knowledge and excellence in the real estate industry and can set this industry on its ear! It is no surprise that associations, organizations, REALTORS® and real estate professionals are lining up across the globe to see her presentations. In the midst of a demanding travel schedule and crafting and delivering powerful education, she so graciously accepted this calling. She is not only a thought leader and expert, but also deeply passionate about making a lifelong difference in the lives of everyone she touches.

I'd like to extend my deepest gratitude to my family. I cannot begin to thank you enough for your unwavering support and encouragement throughout the duration of this project. For being the cheerleader in my corner, reading through my early drafts, advice on color and design, keeping me on track, always listening so intently, and for being my mental break, even when I didn't know I needed one. And especially Mom, my first editor, who helped me to unravel so many story lines, for all the brainstorming conversations, for your insistence that the book was good, and I was good, and I could do it. I would have never come this far without you by my side.

–I love you all.

end notes

Chapter 2:

1. "National Census Of Fatal Occupational Injuries In 2020." Accessed February 8, 2022. https://www.bls.gov/news. release/pdf/cfoi.pdf.

2. "2020 Member Safety Report - National Association of Realtors." Accessed February 9, 2022. https://www.nar. realtor/sites/default/files/documents/2020-member-safety-report-08-31-2020.pdf.

Chapter 3:

1. Sawe, Benjamin Elisha. "The Biggest Industries In The United States." WorldAtlas. WorldAtlas, August 1, 2017. Accessed February 9, 2022. https://www.worldatlas.com/articles/ which-are-the-biggest-industries-in-the-united-states.html.

2. "FBI Releases 2020 Crime Statistics." FBI. FBI, September 27, 2021. Accessed February 9, 2022. https://www.fbi.gov/news/pressrel/press-releases/ fbi-releases-2020-crime-statistics.

3. Farlety, Robert. "Seemingly interested home buyer attacks Realtor." Tampa Bay Times, March 6, 2006. Accessed February 10, 2022. https:// www.tampabay.com/archive/2006/03/06/ seemingly-interested-home-buyer-attacks-realtor/

4. "U.S. Department of Housing and Urban Development …" Accessed February 9, 2022. https://www.hud.gov/sites/ documents/HUD_OGCGUIDAPPFHASTANDCR.PDF.

Chapter 4:

1. Commonwealth v. Yeager, J-S02040-17, (Pa. Super. Ct. Jun. 13, 2017)

Chapter 5:

1. Garner, Erica. "'Creepy' Shed Making Abilene Realtors Uncomfortable." KTAB - BigCountryHomepage. com. KTAB - BigCountryHomepage.com, December 29, 2017. Accessed February 9, 2022. https://www. bigcountryhomepage.com/news/main-news/ creepy-shed-making-abilene-realtors-uncomfortable/.

2. "Real Estate Agent Jim Rudometkin Targeted In Deadly Downey Home-Invasion Robbery." ABC7 Los Angeles. KABC-TV, January 19, 2016. Accessed February 9, 2022. https://abc7.com/downey-home-invasion-robbery-real-estate-agent-jim-rudometkin/1164164/.

Chapter 6:

1. California, Court of Appeals of. "People v. Yates: No. E052576.: 20110826044." Leagle. Court of Appeals of California, Fourth District, Division Two.https://leagle. com/images/logo.png. Accessed February 9, 2022. https:// www.leagle.com/decision/incaco20110826044.

2. California, Court of Appeals of. "People v. Yates: No. E052576.: 20110826044." Leagle. Court of Appeals of California, Fourth District, Division Two. https://leagle. com/images/logo.png. Accessed February 9, 2022. https:// www.leagle.com/decision/incaco20110826044.

3. CBS Los Angeles. "Corona Man Gets 91 Years For Stabbing, Raping And Beating Real Estate Agent." CBS Los Angeles. CBS Los Angeles, December 14, 2010. Accessed February 9, 2022. https://losangeles.cbslocal.com/2010/12/14/corona-man-gets-91-years-for-stabbing-raping-and-beating-real-estate-agent/.

4. "2022 Code of Ethics & Standards of Practice." www.
    nar.realtor. Accessed February 9, 2022. https://www.
    nar.realtor/about-nar/governing-documents/
    code-of-ethics/2021-code-of-ethics-standards-of-
    practice#DutiestoCandC.

Chapter 7:

1. "Caught On Camera: Realtor Attacked During Open House."
    YouTube. Accessed February 9, 2022. https://www.youtube.
    com/watch?v=_hY9Mp2on8k.

Chapter 8:

1. Stimson, Brie. "Virginia Realtor Killed In Murder-Suicide
    By Client Who Just Purchased Home, Police Say." Fox
    News. FOX News Network, October 14, 2021. Accessed
    February 9, 2022. https://www.foxnews.com/us/virginia-
    realtor-killed-in-murder-suicide-by-client-who-just-
    purchased-home-police-say.

2. "Sabor Town Hall Meeting 2011: Janice Tisdale's Story."
    YouTube. Accessed February 9, 2022. https://www.
    youtube.com/watch?v=-BqxxgSWSqQ; Olick, Diana.
    "New Tech Firm Aims to Protect Real Estate Agents
    From Opioid Addicts." CNBC. CNBC, November 13,
    2017. Accessed February 9, 2022. https://www.cnbc.
    com/2017/11/06/new-tech-firm-aims-to-protect-real-
    estate-agents-from-opioid-addicts.html.;Degollado, Jessie.
    "Attack Survivor Urges Realtors To Be On Guard." KSAT.
    KSAT San Antonio, March 23, 2012. Accessed February 9,
    2022. https://www.ksat.com/news/2012/03/23/attack-
    survivor-urges-realtors-to-be-on-guard-2/.;Luz Elena D.
    Chapa, Justice. "Emilio J. Maldonado v. The State of Texas
    Appeal from 290th Judicial District Court of Bexar County
    (Memorandum Opinion)." Justia Law. Accessed February
    9, 2022. https://law.justia.com/cases/texas/fourth-court-
    of-appeals/2013/04-12-00145-cr.html.

3. Sainty, Lane. "Real Estate Agent's 'Gut Feeling' On Killer Dad." news.com.au - Australia's leading news site, May 19, 2021. Accessed February 9, 2022. https://www.news.com.au/national/nsw-act/courts-law/real-estate-agents-gut-feeling-on-killer-dad-john-edwards/news-story/ae956303d8e4cf3b76af1e9cdee8c6e5.;France-Presse, Agence. "Father Kills Teenage Children In Sydney Then Shoots Himself." NDTV.com. NDTV, July 6, 2018. Accessed February 9, 2022. https://www.ndtv.com/world-news/father-commits-suicide-after-murdering-son-and-daughter-in-australia-1878805.

Chapter 9:

1. "2020 Internet Crime Report." Accessed February 9, 2022. https://www.ic3.gov/Media/PDF/AnnualReport/2020_IC3Report.pdf.

2. "Survey: Title Professionals Targeted For Wire Fraud In A Third of All Transactions." ALTA Blog. Accessed February 9, 2022. https://blog.alta.org/2021/04/survey-title-professionals-targeted-for-wire-fraud-in-a-third-of-all-transactions.html.

3. "On The Internet." FBI. FBI, May 3, 2016. Accessed February 9, 2022. https://www.fbi.gov/scams-and-safety/on-the-internet.

Made in the USA
Middletown, DE
26 May 2022

66245530R00104